2021
BOOK OF WORLD RECORDS

BY
CYNTHIA O'BRIEN
ABIGAIL MITCHELL
MICHAEL BRIGHT
DONALD SOMMERVILLE
ANTONIA VAN DER MEER

Due to this book's publication date, the majority of statistics are current as of May 2020. The publisher does not have any control over and does not assume any responsibility for author or third-party websites or their content.

This book was created and produced by Toucan Books Limited.
Text: Cynthia O'Brien, Abigail Mitchell, Michael Bright, Donald Sommerville, Antonia van der Meer
Designer: Lee Riches
Editor: Anna Southgate
Proofreader: Richard Beatty
Index: Marie Lorimer
Toucan would like to thank Cian O'Day for picture research.

ISBN 978-1-338-66605-2

10 9 8 7 6 5 4 3 2   21 22 23 24

Printed in the U.S.A. 40

First printing, 2020

CONTENTS

1

music MAKERS

♫ music makers
trending

TIKTOK BOOM
BTS FANS GO WILD
In 2019, K-Pop sensation BTS became the first TikTok user to reach one million followers. The group joined the app on September 25 and reached the milestone figure in less than four hours. BTS posted two videos—one showing the seven band members greeting fans, captioned "hello, we are BTS!," and another of the group performing three hand gestures to their song "Boy With Luv" for fans to copy.

CUZ THEY LOVE YOU
ENTERTAINER OF THE YEAR
Following a career-making year of feel-good songs and high-energy, flute-wielding performances, singer and rapper Lizzo was named *Time*'s 2019 entertainer of the year. Lizzo was also the year's most nominated artist at the Grammys, with eight nominations that included the high-profile Album of the Year nomination for *Cuz I Love You* and Song of the Year for "Truth Hurts."

#PEACEATLAST
POP RIVALS MAKE UP
Pop superstars Katy Perry and Taylor Swift officially ended their five-year feud when Perry posted a picture of a plate of cookies from Swift's kitchen on Instagram in June 2019. The words "PEACE AT LAST" on the plate, as well as Perry's "Let's Be Friends" location tag, were confirmed to be referring to Swift when Perry tagged her in the caption.

BIEBER'S BACK
SEVEN NO. 1s
Justin Bieber made a comeback in 2020 with his album *Changes*, the first in five years. *Changes* rocketed to no. 1, breaking U.S. chart records to make Bieber the youngest solo artist to have seven albums at no. 1. The Canadian singer was just twenty-five years old at the time. The previous record was held by Elvis Presley, who was twenty-six years old when he set the record in December 1961.

MEME-WORTHY
BILLIE'S ICONIC EXPRESSIONS
The 2020 Academy Awards were noteworthy for an unexpected reason—Billie Eilish's facial expressions! During a presentation by comedians Maya Rudolph and Kristen Wiig, Eilish gained meme-of-the-moment status, as screenshots and GIFs of her incredulous look were gleefully posted by Twitter users as a perfect reaction to all things confusing.

most-streamed song of 2019
"SEÑORITA"

With more than one billion plays on Spotify in 2019, "Señorita" took the crown for the most-streamed song of the year. The duo behind it—Cuban American singer Camila Cabello and Canadian singer-songwriter Shawn Mendes—released their steamy hit on Island Records. The two also snagged a nomination for Best Pop Duo at the 2020 Grammys and took home a Moon Person trophy when "Señorita" won Best Collaboration at the Video Music Awards in August 2019. This is the second time Mendes and Cabello have teamed up to create a single. In 2015, they wrote and sang "I Know What You Did Last Summer," which made it to no. 20 on the charts.

MOST-STREAMED SONGS 2019

Camila Cabello and Shawn Mendes, "Señorita"

Billie Eilish, "bad guy"

Post Malone and Swae Lee, "Sunflower"

Ariana Grande, "7 rings"

Lil Nas X and Billy Ray Cyrus, "Old Town Road—Remix"

top-selling
album
LOVER
Taylor Swift

Taylor Swift does it again! In 2018 she took the title of bestselling album for *Reputation*. This year, she's in the no. 1 spot again with *Lover*, the singer-songwriter's seventh studio album, released in August 2019 by Republic Records. It has already sold more than one million copies. Her hit single "Lover" from the album climbed to no. 10 on the *Billboard* Hot 100.

Taylor Swift can now boast a bestselling album in four different years—*Fearless* in 2009, *1989* in 2014, *Reputation* in 2018, and *Lover* in 2019. This latest album sold 679,000 copies in the first week of sales, giving Swift the distinction of being the first female artist to have six albums that each sold more than 500,000 copies in a single week.

"CON CALMA"
Daddy Yankee & Snow

most-viewed online music video

Puerto Rican singer-songwriter and rapper Daddy Yankee took first place in 2019 on YouTube, thanks to his dance-heavy music video "Con Calma," released in January. With more than 1.8 billion views, it features a crew of high-energy dancers choreographed by Greg Chapkis. The catchy reggaeton song is an updated version of Canadian rapper Snow's 1992 hit "Informer." Snow and Yankee cowrote the new Latin version. Yankee is no stranger to Spanish-language hits. His 2017 single "Despacito" with Luis Fonsi was a smash success—it made the no. 1 spot on the *Billboard* Hot 100, the first all-Spanish language song to do so since "La Macarena" twenty-one years prior.

ED SHEERAN

British singer-songwriter Ed Sheeran has the highest-grossing tour of all time, surpassing those of U2, the Rolling Stones, Guns N' Roses, and Coldplay. Sheeran's tour for his album ÷ (*Divide*) grossed $775.6 million, making it the biggest moneymaker ever for a musical tour. Sheeran's impressive title is no doubt helped by the fact that the tour stretched for longer than two years, beginning in Turin, Italy, in March 2017 and ending in Ipswich, England, in August 2019. By the time it was over, Sheeran had visited forty-three countries and had performed before 8.5 million people.

HIGHEST-GROSSING TOURS EVER
Revenue in millions of U.S. dollars

Ed Sheeran, Divide: 775.6

U2, 360°: 736

Guns N' Roses, Not in This Lifetime . . . : 584

The Rolling Stones, A Bigger Bang: 558

Coldplay, A Head Full of Dreams: 523

first rapper to top
Billboard 100 chart
DRAKE

Drake released his album *If You're Reading This It's Too Late* through iTunes on February 12, 2015. The digital album sold 495,000 units in its first week and entered the *Billboard* 100 at no. 1, making **Drake** the first rap artist ever to top the chart. The album also helped Drake secure another record: the most hits on the *Billboard* 100 at one time.

On March 7, 2015, Drake had fourteen hit songs on the chart, matching the record the Beatles have held since 1964. Since releasing his first hit single, "Best I Ever Had," in 2009, Drake has seen many of his singles go multiplatinum, including "Hotline Bling," which sold 41,000 copies in its first week and had eighteen weeks at no. 1 on the *Billboard* 100.

top group/duo
JONAS BROTHERS

Billboard named American pop-rock band Jonas Brothers as the top group/duo of 2019. Their album *Happiness Begins*—their first in ten years—topped the U.S. *Billboard* 200. The band is made up of three brothers: Kevin, Joe, and Nick. These three talented siblings from New Jersey went from Disney Channel stardom to packed arenas of devoted fans. The trio stopped singing together in 2013, and Nick released two albums on his own (in 2009, he also performed with his side project, Nick Jonas & the Administration). But the boys reunited for this album and are doing better than ever. The group is also the subject of a documentary, called *Chasing Happiness*, about their journey to fame; some say making the film led to the members' decision to get back together.

TOP GROUP/DUOS 2019
1. Jonas Brothers
2. BTS
3. Panic! At the Disco
4. Queen
5. Dan + Shay

top-selling
THE recording group
BEATLES

TOP-SELLING RECORDING GROUPS IN THE UNITED STATES
Albums sold in millions

The Beatles: 183

Garth Brooks: 156

Elvis Presley: 146.5

Eagles: 120

Led Zeppelin: 111.5

The Beatles continue to hold the record for the bestselling recording group in the United States with 183 million albums sold. The British band recorded their first album in September 1962 and made their *Billboard* debut with "I Want to Hold Your Hand." Before breaking up in 1969, the group had twenty number-one songs and recorded some of the world's most famous albums, including *Sgt. Pepper's Lonely Hearts Club Band.*

shortest ever concert
WHITE STRIPES

In St. John's, Newfoundland, the White Stripes's lead, Jack White, played just one note—a C sharp. The White Stripes had played at least one show in each of Canada's thirteen provinces and territories, as well as "secret" shows in various venues. Die-hard fans found out about these secret shows through posts on the White Stripes message board, The Little Room.

The one-note show in Newfoundland was a secret event, though hundreds turned up to watch. The official end of the tour was a full set played later that night. *Under Great White Northern Lights*, released in 2010, is a documentary of the tour. The film features backstage moments as well as scenes from the live concerts, and an impromptu performance on a public bus.

most-streamed
song ever
on Spotify

Ed Sheeran's "Shape of You" broke records in 2018 by becoming the first song to hit two billion streams on Spotify—a feat that also makes it the platform's most-streamed song ever. Originally written by Sheeran for Rihanna, the British singer-songwriter ended up releasing the song himself as part of his album

÷ (*Divide*), to massive success. "Shape of You" officially hit diamond status according to the Recording Industry Association of America in January 2019, meaning that it had achieved ten million units sold (or streaming sales equivalents). It also won Sheeran a Grammy Award in 2018 for Best Pop Solo Performance.

"SHAPE OF YOU"

Ed Sheeran

longest-ever
music video
"HAPPY"
by pharrell

Pharrell Williams made history in November 2013 with the release of the first twenty-four-hour music video—the longest music video ever. The video for Williams's hit song "Happy" is a four-minute track that plays on a loop 360 times. In addition to Williams, celebrities such as Jamie Foxx, Steve Carell, and Miranda Cosgrove make appearances in the video. In 2014, "Happy" broke records again, becoming the first single to top six *Billboard* charts in one year and becoming the year's bestselling song with 6,455,000 digital copies sold.

TAYLOR SWIFT

top-earning female singer

Singer-songwriter Taylor Swift was 2019's top-earning female singer, racking up $185 million gross. How did she do it? By making a number of strategic moves, including reportedly negotiating fairer royalties with Apple Music and cutting a new deal with Spotify. Her seven albums have all gone multiplatinum, but her tours bring her the most income. The first Fearless tour brought in $75 million, while her Reputation tour in 2018 became the highest-grossing U.S. stadium tour of all time. Swift donates to causes and people who are close to her heart, including a $113,000 gift to the Tennessee Equality Project, an LGBTQ advocacy group.

TOP-EARNING FEMALE SINGER
In millions of U.S. dollars

Taylor Swift: 185

Beyoncé: 81

Rihanna: 62

Katy Perry: 57.5

P!nk: 57

"OLD TOWN ROAD"

In 2019 rapper Lil Nas X's "Old Town Road" spent **seventeen** weeks in the no. 1 spot, pushing past "Despacito" from Luis Fonsi and Mariah Carey's "One Sweet Day," each of which spent sixteen **weeks** at the top of the charts. Lil Nas X's real **name** is Montero Hill, and he is from **Atlanta**, Georgia. He recorded the song himself, and **people** first fell in love with the catchy **tune** on the app TikTok. "Old Town Road" made it to the country charts, but it **was** later dropped for not being considered a country song. Disagreements about its genre fueled interest in the song, however, and it subsequently hit no. 1. The song was then remixed and rerecorded with country music star **Billy Ray Cyrus**, who was encouraged to do it by his wife, Tish.

act with the most
Country Music Awards
GEORGE STRAIT

"King of Country" George Strait won his first Country Music Award (CMA) in 1985 for Male Vocalist of the Year and Album of the Year. Since then, Strait has won an amazing twenty-three CMAs, including Entertainer of the Year in 2013. The country music superstar has thirty-three platinum or multiplatinum albums, and he holds the record for the most platinum certifications in country music. George Strait was inducted into the Country Music Hall of Fame in 2006.

musician with the most MTV Video Music Awards
BEYONCÉ

The queen of pop, Beyoncé, is the winningest VMA artist ever. She won eight MTV Video Music Awards in 2016 alone, pushing her ahead of Madonna's twenty VMA trophies and setting a new record of twenty-four VMA wins. The music video for "Formation," from Beyoncé's visual album *Lemonade*, won five awards, including the coveted prize for Video of the Year. With eight Moon Person trophies from eleven nominations, Beyoncé tied the record for the most VMA wins in one year by a female solo artist, also held by Lady Gaga.

MUSICIAN WITH THE MOST MTV VIDEO MUSIC AWARDS

Beyoncé: 24

Madonna: 20

Lady Gaga: 13

Eminem: 13

Peter Gabriel: 12

top country song 2019

"WHISKEY GLASSES"

Morgan Wallen nabbed the no. 1 spot on the *Billboard* Country Airplay chart and Mediabase chart with his song "Whiskey Glasses." It was the third single from his 2019 album *If I Know Me*, and it spent twenty-seven weeks on the *Billboard* Hot 100. It's a cheerful song, despite being about a man whose girlfriend leaves him.

Wallen got his big break with the song "Up Down," which featured Florida Georgia Line. But he's been working his way up since long before then. He appeared on *The Voice* in 2014, making it onto Usher's team and then onto Adam Levine's. He was eliminated in the playoffs, but the setback did nothing to stop his meteoric rise.

TOP COUNTRY SONGS 2019

♫ ♫ ♫ ♫ ♫ Morgan Wallen, "Whiskey Glasses"

♫ ♫ ♫ ♫ Dan + Shay, "Speechless"

♫ ♫ ♫ Blake Shelton, "God's Country"

♫ ♫ Luke Combs, "Beautiful Crazy"

♫ Luke Combs, "Beer Never Broke My Heart"

TAYLOR SWIFT

The awards have been mounting for pop superstar Taylor Swift. The singer-songwriter swept the 2019 American Music Awards by winning six honors—including Artist of the Year and Artist of the Decade. These wins bring her lifetime total to a grand twenty-nine awards, beating Michael Jackson's lifetime record of twenty-four. In celebration, Swift performed a retrospective medley of tunes from throughout her musical career, and she was joined onstage by friends Camila Cabello and Halsey for a performance of "Shake It Off." Her parents were in the audience to share the joy of her accomplishment. Her other music awards include ten Grammys, among them two Albums of the Year, first for *Fearless* and later for *1989*.

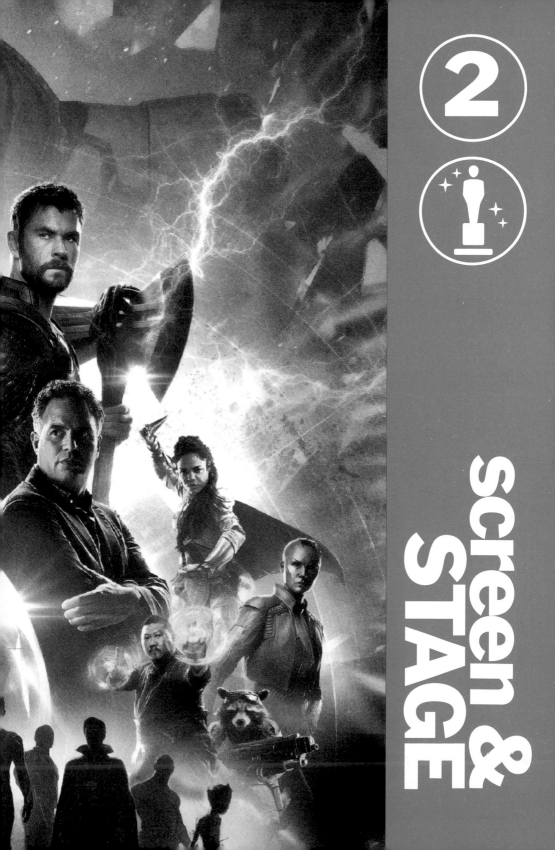

screen & STAGE

screen & stage
trending

THE CHILD IS BORN
"BABY YODA" GOES VIRAL

Following the release of *Star Wars* spin-off *The Mandalorian*, the Internet could not stop talking about its new favorite character "Baby Yoda," named in the series as The Child. The adorable alien charmed social network users with memes of his wide eyes and egg-shaped carrier, and even became popular enough to be made into plush toys for some IRL cuteness.

KING OF THE SCREEN
MOST-STREAMED SHOW ON NETFLIX

According to the streaming giant, the true crime documentary *Tiger King: Murder, Mayhem, and Madness* was its most-watched title for a record sixteen days in a row. Directed by Louis Theroux, the program fascinated viewers with tales of American big-cat owners and breeders, their feuds, and crimes—and Joe Exotic's outlandish accusation that Carole Baskin had fed her husband to her tigers!

A WHOLE NEW WORLD
NEW STREAMING SERVICE

2019 saw the launch of Disney+, a streaming platform for Disney's back catalog of movies, shorts, and shows, plus a host of exclusive new content. This includes not only Disney and Pixar gems but also content from ESPN, Marvel, and Star Wars—including the platform's new show *The Mandalorian*. Disney+ now has more than fifty million paid subscribers globally.

INTO THE UNKNOWN
BIGGEST OPENING WEEKEND

In November 2019, *Frozen II* smashed the record for highest opening weekend earnings for an animated movie, previously held by *Toy Story 4*. The sequel made $358 million in its first three days, opening in thirty-seven countries. The first *Frozen* film, which introduced the beloved characters of Elsa, Anna, Olaf, and Sven, still holds the record for the highest-earning animated film ever at $1.27 billion in box office sales, as well as the revenue from its popular merchandise.

BOX-OFFICE FLOP
TOO WEIRD TO LOVE

The movie adaption of Andrew Lloyd Webber's musical *Cats* featured the likes of Taylor Swift and Jennifer Hudson donning skintight, hairless catsuits and participating in fantastical song-and-dance numbers. The film cost $100 million to make but opened to just $6.5 million in the United States, thanks to viewers' public criticisms.

longest-running
scripted TV show in the United States THE
SIMPSONS

MATT GROENING

In 2019, *The Simpsons* entered a record thirty-first season, continuing to hold the title of longest-running American sitcom, cartoon, and scripted prime-time television show in history. The animated comedy, which first aired in December 1989, centers on the antics and everyday lives of the Simpson family. Famous guest stars who have made appearances over the years range from Stephen Hawking to Kelsey Grammer and Ed Sheeran (as Lisa's new crush). Fox has renewed the show for the upcoming thirty-second season, too.

FLEABAG

The quirky, two-season tragicomedy *Fleabag* walked away from the 2019 Emmy Awards with six statues including for Comedy Series; Lead Actress, Comedy Series; Writing, Comedy Series; and Directing, Comedy Series. British phenom Phoebe Waller-Bridge earned kudos as the show's creator, writer, and lead actress. The series was created for the BBC but later aired in the United States on Amazon Prime. The show—both funny and heartbreaking—is about a young single woman's struggle with life, loss, love, depression, and strained family relationships. The format is unusual because the main character often speaks directly to the TV audience, breaking the "fourth wall" to offer remarks. Waller-Bridge says the second season was the end and there are no plans for a third season.

highest-paid TV actress SOFÍA VERGARA

Sofía Vergara holds top spot for the highest-paid TV actress in 2019, earning $44.1 million. Much of her income is down to her role as Gloria Delgado-Pritchett on *Modern Family*, which drew to a close in April 2020 after an amazing eleven seasons. Almost half of it comes from endorsements and licensing deals that include coffee maker SharkNinja Coffee and furniture chain Rooms To Go. Originally from Colombia, Vergara won four Screen Actors Guild Awards as part of the *Modern Family* cast for Outstanding Performance by an Ensemble in a Comedy Series.

TOP-EARNING TV ACTRESSES
In millions of U.S. dollars

Sofía Vergara: 44.1

Kaley Cuoco: 25

Elisabeth Moss: 24

Charlize Theron: 23

Ellen Pompeo: 22

most-popular
original Netflix
show of 2019

STRANGER THINGS 3

MOST POPULAR ORIGINAL NETFLIX SERIES OF 2019
1. *Stranger Things 3*
2. *The Witcher*
3. *The Umbrella Academy*
4. *Dead to Me*
5. *You: Season 2*

There was much binge-worthy content on Netflix this year. But what kept people glued to their screens more than any other show was *Stranger Things 3*. Fans loved the third season of this otherworldly story of kids battling demons in a small town in Indiana in the early 1980s. Created by the Duffer Brothers, it has been a runaway hit since season one was released in 2016. The twisty science fiction plot begins when young Will disappears and his friends must fight supernatural forces to find him. In the third season, it's summer and the kids are together again to fight the evil that lurks beneath them. The season ends with an epic battle in the new mall's food court.

most-watched television broadcast of 2019

SUPER BOWL LIII

The most-watched television broadcast of 2019 was Super Bowl LIII. More than ninety-eight million viewers tuned in to watch the Patriots beat the Rams 13–3. That's a lot of eyeballs, but it's still about five percent fewer than the TV audience for the 2018 Super Bowl. Streaming coverage made up for the loss in traditional TV viewers. The live stream was available on CBS's subscription service, CBS All Access. The game was the first Super Bowl ever without a touchdown going into the fourth quarter. The rivals scored only six total points during the first three quarters, the fewest in Super Bowl history, according to ESPN.

JIM PARSONS

Jim Parsons was yet again TV's highest-paid actor in 2019, earning $26.5 million. Most of his income came from playing television's favorite physicist, Sheldon Cooper, on *The Big Bang Theory*. His costars Johnny Galecki, Simon Helberg, and Kunal Nayyar also made the top five. Fans had to say goodbye to the sitcom in May 2019, with a finale that boasted nearly twenty-five million viewers. Parsons will remain connected to the show's success, as he will continue to narrate and help produce CBS's *Big Bang* prequel, *Young Sheldon*.

HIGHEST-PAID TV ACTORS
In millions of U.S. dollars

Jim Parsons: 26.5	Johnny Galecki: 25	Simon Helberg: 23.5	Kunal Nayyar: 23.5	Mark Harmon: 19

most successful
movie franchise

MARVEL CINEMATIC UNIVERSE

The Marvel Cinematic Universe franchise has grossed more than $18.26 billion worldwide—and counting! This impressive total includes ticket sales from the huge hits of 2018, *Black Panther* and *Avengers: Infinity War*. *Black Panther* grossed $1.34 billion worldwide within three months of its release, but then *Avengers: Infinity War* hit the screens, taking $1.82 billion worldwide in its first month. With *Avengers: Endgame* earning even greater revenues in 2019, the Marvel Cinematic Universe looks set to hold this record for the foreseeable future.

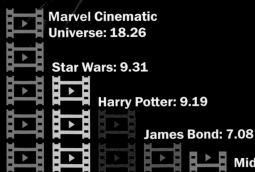

Marvel Cinematic Universe: 18.26

Star Wars: 9.31

Harry Potter: 9.19

James Bond: 7.08

Middle-Earth: 5.89

MOST SUCCESSFUL MOVIE FRANCHISES
Total worldwide gross, in billions of U.S. dollars (as of March 2020)

movies with the most OSCARS

MOVIES WITH THE MOST OSCARS

Ben-Hur (1959): 11

Titanic (1997): 11

The Lord of the Rings: The Return of the King (2003): 11

West Side Story (1961): 10

Gigi (1958); The Last Emperor (1987); The English Patient (1996): 9

It's a three-way tie for the movie with the most Academy Awards: *Ben-Hur*, *Titanic*, and The *Lord of the Rings: The Return of the King* have each won eleven Oscars, including Best Picture and Best Director. The 1959 biblical epic *Ben-Hur* was the first to achieve this record number of wins. *Titanic*, based on the real 1912 disaster, won numerous Oscars for its striking visual and sound effects. *The Lord of the Rings: The Return of the King* was the third in a trilogy based on the books by J. R. R. Tolkien. It is the only movie of the top three to win in every category in which it was nominated.

WHO'S OSCAR?

Every year, the Academy of Motion Picture Arts and Sciences presents awards in recognition of the greatest achievements in the film industry. Those actors, directors, screenwriters, and producers lucky enough to win each receive a highly prized golden statuette, aka "Oscar." No one really knows where the name comes from, although it is thought to have originated among the Hollywood greats of the 1930s—Bette Davis and Walt Disney have been credited, among others. Either way, "Oscar" became the official nickname for the Academy Award in 1939.

youngest actress nominated for an Oscar, QUVENZHANÉ WALLIS

At nine years old, Quvenzhané Wallis became the youngest-ever Academy Award nominee. The actress received the Best Actress nomination in 2013 for her role as Hushpuppy in *Beasts of the Southern Wild*. Although Wallis did not win the Oscar, she went on to gain forty-one more nominations and win twenty-four awards at various industry award shows. In 2015, she received a Golden Globe Best Actress nomination for her role in *Annie*. Wallis was five years old when she auditioned for Hushpuppy (the minimum age was six), and she won the part over four thousand other candidates.

Justin Henry was just seven years old when he received a Best Supporting Actor nomination for *Kramer vs. Kramer* in 1980. His neighbor, a casting director, suggested that Henry try out for the part. Although the young actor lost out on the Oscar, *Kramer vs. Kramer* won several Oscars, including Best Actor for Dustin Hoffman, Best Actress in a Supporting Role for Meryl Streep, and Best Picture. Justin Henry appeared in a few other films before leaving acting to finish his education. He then returned to acting in the 1990s.

youngest
actor
nominated
for an Oscar
JUSTIN
HENRY

movie with the most successful

domestic opening weekend

AVENGERS: ENDGAME

WORLDWIDE *AVENGERS* OPENING WEEKENDS:

$1.2 billion
AVENGERS: ENDGAME (2019)

$640.5 million
AVENGERS: INFINITY WAR (2018)

$392.5 million
AVENGERS: AGE OF ULTRON (2015)

Avengers: Endgame broke the record set by *Avengers: Infinity War* to become the movie with the most successful opening weekend ever in the United States. On its release in April 2019, *Endgame* took an astonishing $357 million in its opening weekend in the United States. *Infinity War*, its chronological Marvel Cinematic Universe (MCU) predecessor, took home $257.6 on its own opening weekend—an impressive number, even if it was nearly $100 million less than *Endgame*. *Endgame* made box-office history with a record-breaking $1.2 billion sales worldwide in its opening run. It represents the finale to phase three of the MCU series, which at the time encompassed twenty-two movies.

actresses with the most
MTV Movie Awards
JENNIFER LAWRENCE
AND KRISTEN STEWART

ACTRESSES WITH THE MOST MTV MOVIE AWARDS

★★★★★ Jennifer Lawrence: 7

★★★★★ Kristen Stewart: 7

★★★ Shailene Woodley: 5

★★★ Sandra Bullock: 5

★★ Alicia Silverstone: 4

Jennifer Lawrence and Kristen Stewart share the title of actress with the most MTV Movie Awards. Stewart won all seven of her awards for her role as Bella Swan in the movie adaptations of the Twilight franchise—including four Best Kiss awards with costar Robert Pattinson. Lawrence's seventh award was for Best Hero, which she won in 2016 for her role as Katniss Everdeen in the fourth installment of the popular Hunger Games franchise. The actress, however, was a no-show at the awards ceremony that year, due to press commitments for her upcoming movie X-Men: Apocalypse.

actor with the most
JIM CARREY
MTV Movie Awards

Jim Carrey has eleven MTV Movie Awards, including five Best Comedic Performance awards for his roles in *Dumb and Dumber* (1994), *Ace Ventura: When Nature Calls* (1995), *The Cable Guy* (1996), *Liar Liar* (1997), and *Yes Man* (2008). He won the Best Villain award twice, once for *The Cable Guy* (1996) and the second time for *Dr. Seuss' How the Grinch Stole Christmas* (2000). Fans also awarded Carrey with the Best Kiss award for his lip-lock with Lauren Holly in *Dumb and Dumber*.

ACTORS WITH THE MOST MTV MOVIE AWARDS

★★★★★ Jim Carrey: 11

★★★★ Robert Pattinson: 10

★★★ Mike Myers: 7

★ Adam Sandler: 6

★ Will Smith: 6

SCARLETT JOHANSSON

top-earning actress

The highest-paid film actress of 2019 was Scarlett Johansson, who earned $56 million before tax—almost forty percent more than her previous year's earnings. Johansson has been receiving increasingly high paydays for movies within the expanding Marvel Cinematic Universe. Johansson plays the Black Widow Natasha Romanoff in the superhero franchise. Johansson is not the only film actress to make considerably more than she did last year. Reese Witherspoon saw her earnings more than double from 16.5 million in 2018 to 35 million in 2019.

TOP-EARNING ACTRESSES OF 2019
In millions of U.S. dollars

Scarlett Johansson: 56

Reese Witherspoon: 35

Nicole Kidman: 34

Jennifer Aniston: 28

Margot Robbie: 23.5

top-earning
actor
THE ROCK

According to *Forbes*, Dwayne "The Rock" Johnson earned a cool $89.4 million pretax in 2019, making him the top-earning actor. The big bucks can be chalked up to the star's huge social media following, which enables financial deals outside of his acting career. Plus, he has clothing and shoe lines for Under Armour. Even with all the extra side businesses, the Rock earns most of his money from acting. He was paid $23.5 million upfront for 2019's *Jumanji: The Next Level*, and he makes $700,000 per episode for *Ballers* on HBO.

TOP-EARNING ACTORS OF 2019
In millions of U.S. dollars

The Rock: 89.4

Chris Hemsworth: 76.4

Robert Downey Jr.: 66

Akshay Kumar: 65

Jackie Chan: 58

top-grossing movie
AVENGERS: ENDGAME

Avengers: Endgame was the top-grossing movie of the year, with more than $858 million at the box office. The film's release in April came just seven weeks after the release of *Captain Marvel*, the twenty-first film in the Marvel Cinematic Universe franchise, which also climbed the chart to the fifth-highest gross for the year. *Captain Marvel* stars Brie Larson in the title role and is the first film of the franchise to feature a female lead in its name. It is also the first film ever with a female lead (and female director) to gross $1 billion. *Avengers: Endgame* sold a staggering ninety-four million tickets to earn its place at the top of the list.

TOP-GROSSING MOVIES OF 2019
Gross in millions of U.S. dollars

Avengers: Endgame: $858

The Lion King: $544

Frozen II: $450

Toy Story 4: $434

Captain Marvel: $427

animated-film franchise

DESPICABLE ME

Following the hugely successful 2017 release of the third movie in the series, *Despicable Me 3*, and with a global total of $3.528 billion, Despicable Me became the world's highest-grossing animated franchise of all time. The 2015 spin-off *Minions* is the most profitable animated film in Universal Studios' history and was the highest-grossing film of the year, while *Despicable Me 3* and Oscar-nominated *Despicable Me 2* hit spot no. 2 in their respective years of release. Collectively the four movies beat the Shrek franchise's takings of $3.51 billion, a total that includes sales from the spin-off *Puss in Boots*.

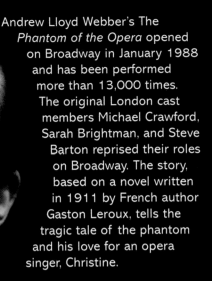

longest-running Broadway show

Andrew Lloyd Webber's The *Phantom of the Opera* opened on Broadway in January 1988 and has been performed more than 13,000 times. The original London cast members Michael Crawford, Sarah Brightman, and Steve Barton reprised their roles on Broadway. The story, based on a novel written in 1911 by French author Gaston Leroux, tells the tragic tale of the phantom and his love for an opera singer, Christine.

THE PHANTOM OF THE OPERA

LONGEST-RUNNING BROADWAY SHOWS
Total performances (as of May 2020)

The Phantom of the Opera: **13,370**

Chicago (1996 revival): **9,692**

The Lion King: **9,302**

Cats: **7,485**

Les Misérables: **6,680**

highest-grossing
Broadway musical

THE LION KING

Since opening on November 13, 1997, *The Lion King* has earned $1.7 billion. It's Broadway's third-longest-running production and is an adaptation of the hugely popular Disney animated film. Along with hit songs from the movie such as "Circle of Life" and "Hakuna Matata," the show includes new compositions by South African composer Lebo M. and others. The Broadway show features songs in six African languages, including Swahili and Congolese. Since it opened, *The Lion King* has attracted audiences totaling over one hundred million people.

musical with the most Tony Award nominations
HAMILTON

Lin-Manuel Miranda's musical biography of Founding Father Alexander Hamilton racked up an amazing sixteen Tony Award nominations to unseat the previous record holders, *The Producers* and *Billy Elliot: The Musical*, both of which had fifteen. The mega-hit hip-hop musical, which was inspired by historian Ron Chernow's biography of the first secretary of the treasury, portrays the Founding Fathers of the United States engaging in rap battles over issues such as the national debt and the French Revolution. *Hamilton* won eleven Tonys at the 2016 ceremony—one shy of *The Producers*, which retains the record for most Tony wins with twelve. *Hamilton's* Broadway success paved the way for the show to open in Chicago in 2016, with a touring show and a London production following in 2017.

youngest winner
of a Laurence
Olivier Award

In 2012, four actresses shared an Olivier Award for their roles in the British production of *Matilda*. Eleanor Worthington-Cox, Cleo Demetriou, Kerry Ingram, and Sophia Kiely all won the award for Best Actress in a Musical. Of the four actresses, Worthington-Cox, age ten, was the youngest by a few weeks. Each actress portraying Matilda performs two shows a week. In the United States, the four *Matilda* actresses won a special Tony Honors for Excellence in the Theatre in 2013. *Matilda*, inspired by the book by Roald Dahl, won a record seven Olivier Awards in 2012.

eleanor worthington-cox

cleo demetriou

kerry ingram

sophia kiely

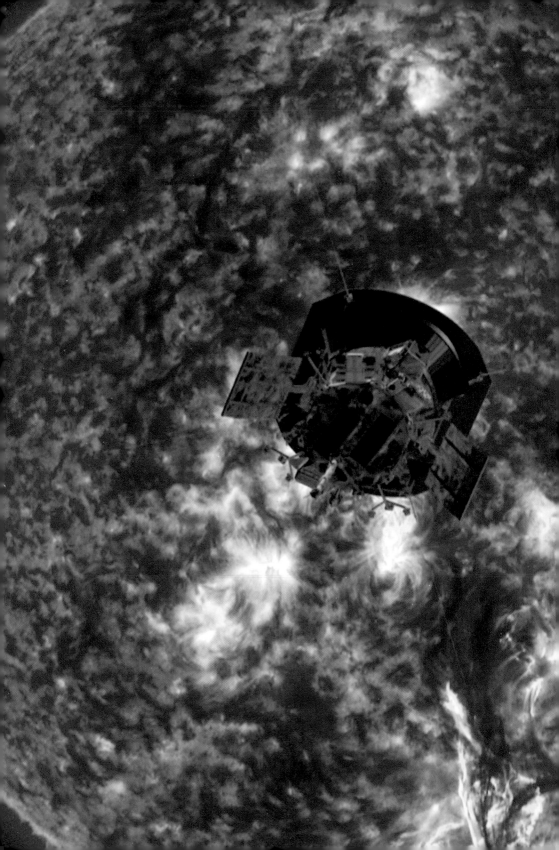

on the
MOVE

on the move
trending

QUICK CHANGE
FASTEST PIT STOP
Aston Martin Red Bull Racing broke the record for the fastest F1 pit stop three times in 2019—first at the British Grand Prix, next at the German Grand Prix, and then at Interlagos, the Brazilian Grand Prix. The pit crew of Dutch driver Max Verstappen's RB15 pulled off an incredible 1.82-second change. Red Bull now plans to challenge its pit crew with a pit change in zero gravity!

DEMO
ULTRA-HARD 30X COLD-ROLLED STAINLESS STEEL

SMASH FAIL
CYBERTRUCK DEMO GOES VIRAL
A video of Tesla CEO and engineer Elon Musk's "Cybertruck" went viral in 2019 when a live demonstration didn't quite go to plan. Musk had described the windows of the Cybertruck as having "armored glass" that was like "transparent metal," but the material proved not to be indestructible. Musk's surprise when the windows were easily cracked by a steel ball prompted viewers to share the video of Tesla's epic fail.

FAR SIDE OF THE MOON

CHINA'S HISTORIC LANDING

On January 2, 2019, Chinese lunar probe Chang'e-4 made a historic landing on the moon's far side, in the Von Kármán Crater. (Because it takes the same amount of time for the moon to spin on its axis as it does for it to orbit Earth, we on Earth only ever see one side of it.) Thanks to the photographs being transmitted by the probe's robot via a relay satellite launched in 2019, scientists are now seeing clear images of this previously unexplored lunar landscape.

HELLO, PERSEVERANCE

NAMING THE NEW ROVER

NASA's new Mars rover, scheduled for launch in 2020, was named *Perseverance* in 2019 following a national essay contest. A total of 28,000 students submitted short essays with their suggestions for a name for the rover, and more than 770,000 voters chose their favorite in an online poll. The winning name was suggested by seventh-grader Alex Mather from Springfield, Virginia, as a reflection of the important characteristic that both the rover and humans possess.

ELECTRO-LUXE

THE LUXURY ELECTRIC CAR

British manufacturer Aston Martin unveiled its first-ever electric car at the 2019 Shanghai Motor Show. The car in question, the Rapide E, will not be mass-produced, but Aston Martin is also working on an all-electric production-ready Lagonda line, with electric cars that will be able to drive themselves.

world's first MONSTER SCHOOL BUS

"Bad to the Bone" is the first monster school bus in the world. This revamped 1956 yellow bus is 13 feet tall, thanks to massive tires with 25-inch rims. The oversize bus weighs 19,000 pounds and is a favorite ride at charity events in California. But don't expect to get anywhere in a hurry—this "Kool Bus" is not built for speed and goes at a maximum of just 7 miles per hour.

most expensive street-legal car
LA VOITURE NOIRE

In February 2019, La Voiture Noire (The Black Car) claimed the crown as the world's most expensive car after being sold for $12.5 million. Only one of these cars was produced by luxury French supercar maker Bugatti, in celebration of its 110th anniversary. Said to take inspiration from the manufacturer's Type 57 SC Atlantic of the 1930s, as well as Darth Vader from *Star Wars*, the car features a sleek, all-black design with six tail pipes. At top speed, this exclusive vehicle can hit 261 miles per hour and can reach 62 miles per hour in 2.4 seconds.

MOST EXPENSIVE CARS
(as of 2019) In U.S. dollars

$$$$$ **Bugatti La Voiture Noire:** $12.5 million

$$$$$ **Rolls-Royce Sweptail:** $10.5 million

$$$$ **Koenigsegg CCXR Trevita:** $4.8 million

$$$$ **Lamborghini Veneno:** $4.5 million

$$$ **McLaren P1M:** $3.6 million

SIN CITY HUSTLER

world's longest monster truck

Measuring 32 feet in length, 12 feet tall, and weighing 15,000 pounds, the Sin City Hustler is the world's longest monster truck. To put that into perspective, its measurements rival those of a *Tyrannosaurus rex*! The truck was custom-built by Brad and Jen Campbell of Big Toyz Racing in White Hills, Arizona, and currently resides in Las Vegas, Nevada. There, it is used as a tourist attraction. Twelve passengers can climb on board for the wildest drive of their lives!

world's smallest trailer
QTVAN

The tiny QTvan is just over 7 feet long, 2.5 feet wide, and 5 feet tall. Inside, however, it has a full-size single bed, a kettle for boiling water, and a 19-inch TV. The Environmental Transport Association (ETA) in Britain sponsored the invention of the minitrailer, which was designed to be pulled by a mobility scooter. The ETA recommends the QTvan for short trips only, since mobility scooters have a top speed of 6 miles per hour, at best.

The world's fastest car is the Thrust SSC, which reached a speed of 763 miles per hour on October 15, 1997, in the Black Rock Desert, Nevada. *SSC* stands for supersonic (faster than the speed of sound). The Thrust SSC's amazing speed comes from two jet engines with 110,000 brake horsepower. That's as much as 145 Formula One race cars. The British-made car uses about 5 gallons of jet fuel in one second and takes just five seconds to reach its top speed. At that speed, the Thrust SSC could travel from New York City to San Francisco in less than four hours. More recently, another British manufacturer has developed a new supersonic car, the Bloodhound, with a projected speed of 1,000 miles per hour. If it reaches that, it will set a new world record.

fastest land vehicle THRUST SSC

fastest
passenger train
SHANGHAI
MAGLEV

The Shanghai Maglev, which runs between Shanghai Pudong International Airport and the outskirts of Shanghai, is the fastest passenger train in the world. The service reaches 268 miles per hour, covering the 19-mile distance in seven minutes and twenty seconds. *Maglev* is short for magnetic levitation, as the train moves by floating on magnets rather than with wheels on a track. Other high-speed trains, such as Japan's SCMaglev, may have reached higher speeds in testing (375 miles per hour), but are capped at 200 miles per hour when carrying passengers.

FASTEST PASSENGER TRAINS
(maximum operating speed)

Shanghai Maglev: 268 mph

China Harmony: 236 mph

Italy Italo: 224 mph

Spain Velaro: 217 mph

Spain Talgo 350: 217 mph

In June 2016, World Supersport rider Kenan Sofuoğlu set a new land-speed record for a production motorcycle—that is, a mass-produced, road-worthy, two-wheeled motorcycle. He reached a top speed of 249 miles per hour in just twenty-six seconds. He was riding the Kawasaki Ninja H2R, currently the fastest production motorcycle in the world, while crossing the Osman Gazi Bridge in Turkey. At 8,799 feet across, this is the world's fourth-longest suspension bridge. The Ninja H2R is currently legal for track racing only, and while Kawasaki produces a street-legal Ninja, it is not the world's fastest. That honor goes to the Madmax Streetfighter, which has a top speed of 233 miles per hour.

fastest production motorcycle KAWASAKI NINJA H2R

largest cruise ship
ROYAL
CARIBBEAN
Symphony of the Seas

With a gross tonnage of 230,000 tons, the new Royal Caribbean cruise ship *Symphony of the Seas* holds the record for the world's largest. It beats 2018's record holder, the 226,963-GT *Harmony of the Seas*, also a Royal Caribbean ship. *Symphony of the Seas* has 2,774 cabins and can carry 5,535 guests at full capacity. The two-story Ultimate Family Suite has an air-hockey table, a LEGO® climbing wall, and a private 3-D movie room with a library of video games and its own popcorn machine.

WORLD'S LARGEST CRUISE SHIPS
Gross tonnage (in tons)

Symphony of the Seas, **Royal Caribbean: 230,000**

Harmony of the Seas, **Royal Caribbean: 226,963**

Allure of the Seas, **Royal Caribbean: 225,282**

Oasis of the Seas, **Royal Caribbean: 225,282**

AIDANova, **Meyer Werft: 184,000**

fastest
helicopter
circumnavigation
of Earth

JENNIFER
MURRAY AND
COLIN BODILL

In 2007, British pilots Jennifer Murray and Colin Bodill became the first pilots ever to fly around the world in a helicopter via the North and South Poles. They also set the record for the fastest time to complete this journey, at 170 days, 22 hours, 47 minutes, and 17 seconds. The pair began and ended their record-setting journey in Fort Worth, Texas, and flew a Bell 407 helicopter. The journey, which began on December 5, 2006, and ended on May 23, 2007, was the duo's second attempt at the record. The first, in 2003, ended with an emergency rescue after they crashed in Antarctica.

lightest jet BD-5J MICROJET

In 2004, the BD-5J Microjet, a one-seater aircraft, secured the record as the world's lightest jet. The jet weighs 358.8 pounds, has a 17-foot wingspan, and is only 12 feet long. Engineer Jim Bede introduced the microjet in the early 1970s and sold hundreds in kit form, ready for self-assembly. The BD-5J model became a popular airshow attraction and was featured in a James Bond movie. The microjet uses a TRS-18 turbojet engine and can carry only 32 gallons of fuel. Its top speed is 300 miles per hour.

fastest unmanned plane X-43A

In November 2004, NASA launched its experimental X-43A plane for a test flight over the Pacific Ocean. The X-43A plane reached Mach 9.6, which is more than nine times the speed of sound and nearly 7,000 miles per hour. A B-52B aircraft carried the X-43A and a Pegasus rocket booster into the air, releasing them at 40,000 feet. At that point, the booster—essentially a fuel-packed engine—ignited, blasting the unmanned X-43A higher and faster, before separating from the plane. The plane continued to fly for several minutes at 110,000 feet, before crashing (intentionally) into the ocean.

fastest man-made object

PARKER SOLAR PROBE

On October 29, 2018, the Parker Solar Probe broke a record that had not been beaten since 1976. Traveling at 155,959 miles per hour, it became the fastest man-made object ever known. Jointly operated by NASA and the Johns Hopkins University, and equipped with a wide range of scientific equipment, the Parker Solar Probe was on a mission to travel as close to the Sun as possible. The day after breaking the speed record, the probe had reached a distance of 25,072,700 miles from the Sun's surface—the closest a spacecraft has ever been. Withstanding extreme heat and radiation, the probe will study the Sun's atmosphere, sending data and images back to Earth, revolutionizing our understanding of the star at the heart of our solar system.

APOLLO 10 FLIGHT STATS

05/18/69

12:49

LAUNCH DATE: May 18, 1969

LAUNCH TIME: 12:49 p.m. EDT

05/21/69

ENTERED LUNAR ORBIT: May 21, 1969

192:03:23

DURATION OF MISSION: 192 hours, 3 minutes, 23 seconds

05/26/69

12:52

RETURN DATE: May 26, 1969

SPLASHDOWN: 12:52 p.m. EDT

fastest manned spacecraft
APOLLO 10

NASA's *Apollo 10* spacecraft reached its top speed on its descent to Earth, hurtling through the atmosphere at 24,816 miles per hour and splashing down on May 26, 1969. The spacecraft's crew had traveled faster than anyone on Earth. The mission was a "dress rehearsal" for the first moon landing by *Apollo 11*, two months later. The *Apollo 10* spacecraft consisted of a Command Service Module, called Charlie Brown, and a Lunar Module, called Snoopy. Today, Charlie Brown is on display at the Science Museum in London, England.

LIFT-OFF
The *Apollo 10* spacecraft was launched from Cape Canaveral, known as Cape Kennedy at the time. It was the fourth manned Apollo launch in seven months.

fastest
roller coaster
FORMULA
ROSSA

FASTEST ROLLER COASTERS

 **Formula Rossa, Abu Dhabi, UAE: 149.1 mph**

 Kingda Ka, New Jersey, USA: 128 mph

Top Thrill Dragster, Ohio, USA: 120 mph

Dodonpa, Yamanashi, Japan: 112 mph

Red Force, Ferrari Land, Tarragona, Spain: 112 mph

FORMULA ROSSA
World Records
Speed: 149.1 mph
G-force: 1.7 Gs
Acceleration: 4.8 Gs

Thrill seekers hurtle along the Formula Rossa track at 149.1 miles per hour. The high-speed roller coaster is part of Ferrari World in Abu Dhabi, United Arab Emirates. Ferrari World also features the world's largest indoor theme park, at 1.5 million square feet. The Formula Rossa roller coaster seats are red Ferrari-shaped cars that travel from 0 to 62 miles per hour in just two seconds—as fast as a race car. The ride's G-force is so extreme that passengers must wear goggles to protect their eyes. G-force acts on a body due to acceleration and gravity. People can withstand 6 to 8 Gs for short periods. The Formula Rossa G-force is 4.8 Gs during acceleration and 1.7 Gs at maximum speed.

tallest water coaster

MASSIV

Schlitterbahn Galveston Island Waterpark in Texas is home to the world's tallest water coaster. The aptly named MASSIV measures in at 81 feet and 6.72 inches tall. A water coaster is a water slide that features ascents as well as descents, with riders traveling in rafts or tubes. MASSIV, which the park calls a "monster blaster," was built for the tenth anniversary of the opening of Schlitterbahn Galveston. Riders sit in two-person tubes, which take them over a series of dips and four uphill climbs before dropping into the final landing pool. In April 2016, the park released a virtual version of the ride, allowing people all over the world to see MASSIV from the point of view of a rider.

CIRCUS

oldest
merry-go-round
FLYING HORSES CAROUSEL

Taking a spin around the Flying Horses Carousel in Martha's Vineyard is a trip back in time. Charles Dare constructed the carousel in 1876 for an amusement park in Coney Island, New York. The carousel moved to Oak Bluffs, Massachusetts, in 1884. A preservation society took over Flying Horses in 1986 to restore the carousel and keep it intact and working. Today, the horses look just as colorful as they did in the 1800s. Their manes are real horsehair, and they have glass eyes. As the horses turn around and around, a 1923 Wurlitzer Band Organ plays old-time music. The Flying Horses Carousel is a National Landmark.

largest
tunnel-boring machine
HERRENKNECHT
S-880

Fitted with a 57.7-foot-diameter cutting head, the Herrenknecht S-880 was used to bore a massive feeder tunnel in Hong Kong, which holds three lanes of traffic. At depths of up to 164 foot, the tunnel is a key section of a 3.1-mile-long twin-tube road-tunnel system for a sea crossing in the Pearl River delta. It is part of a network that seeks to provide better connections between three main areas of Hong Kong: Northwest New Territories, North Lantau, and Hong Kong International Airport. Eventually the network will extend to the Hong Kong-Zhuhai-Macao Bridge system, which was completed in 2018 and is the world's longest sea crossing.

super
STRUCTURES

super structures
trending

SMALL-SCALE LIVING
TINY HOUSE TREND CONTINUES

Tiny houses continued to be a hot topic in 2019, with more people exploring them as a solution to housing crises and overly expensive homes. Plenty of new start-ups got in on the tiny house trend, from one that 3D-prints tiny house neighborhoods for poor residents in Mexico to those creating futuristic pods far from densely populated areas.

NOTRE DAME BURNS
IMAGES SPREAD FAR AND WIDE

Paris mourned on April 15, 2019, when its landmark cathedral, Notre Dame, became engulfed in a fire that destroyed its spire and most of its roof. Images of the blaze spread quickly on social media, and people around the world watched. French video game developer and publisher Ubisoft was flooded with positive reviews after it pledged €500,000 ($620,000 U.S.) toward the cathedral's restoration.

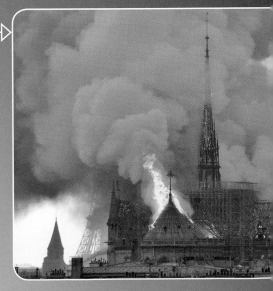

FLOWER POWER
LARGEST FLORAL ARCHITECTURAL SCULPTURE

A whopping 74,000 pots of flowers went into building a castle that was officially named the world's biggest floral architectural sculpture! Completed in about seventy days, the masterpiece is 123 feet 6 inches long, 85 feet 5 inches wide, and 76 feet 11 inches tall. It was created by Anren Overseas Chinese Town Jin Xiu Anren Flower Park, in Chengdu, China.

CLIMATE-PROOF HOMES
THE MERITS OF FLOATING VILLAGES

In 2019, Western planners looked to floating villages as a possible solution to rising waters caused by climate change. Floating cities and their infrastructures are being designed by architects collaborating with the Center for Ocean Engineering at the Massachusetts Institute of Technology, and have been described as both "climate-proof" and "future-proof."

LONDON CALLING
MOST INSTAGRAMMED CITY

The British capital beat out 2018's champion, Paris, to become 2019's most Instagrammed city. It was hashtagged on Instagram photographs 118,539,020 times. The greatest percentages of those photos are group shots (22.5 percent), pictures of the city's best bites (22 percent), and selfies (17 percent).

skyscrapers in the world
HONG KONG

Hong Kong, China, has 355 buildings that reach 500 feet or higher, and one more under construction. Six are 980 feet or higher. The tallest three are the International Commerce Centre (ICC) at 1,588 feet; Two International Finance Centre at 1,352 feet; and Central Plaza at 1,227 feet. Hong Kong's stunning skyline towers above Victoria Harbour. Most of its tallest buildings are on Hong Kong Island, although the other side of the harbor, Kowloon, is growing. Every night a light, laser, and sound show called "A Symphony of Lights" illuminates the sky against a backdrop of about forty of Hong Kong's skyscrapers.

CITIES WITH THE MOST SKYSCRAPERS IN THE WORLD
Number of skyscrapers at 500 feet or higher

Hong Kong, China: 355

New York City, New York, USA: 284

Shenzhen, China: 283

Dubai, UAE: 200

largest
sports stadium
RUNGRADO MAY FIRST STADIUM

It took over two years to build Rungrado May First Stadium, a gigantic sports venue that seats up to 114,000 people. The 197-foot-tall stadium opened in 1989 on Rungra Island in North Korea's capital, Pyongyang. The stadium hosts international soccer matches on its natural grass pitch and has other facilities such as an indoor swimming pool; training halls; and a 1,312-foot rubberized running track. The annual Arirang Festival for gymnastics and arts also takes place here.

LARGEST SPORTS STADIUMS
By capacity

Rungrado May First Stadium, North Korea: 114,000

Michigan Stadium, Michigan, USA: 107,601

Beaver Stadium, Pennsylvania, USA: 106,572

Ohio Stadium, Ohio, USA: 104,944

Kyle Field, Texas, USA: 102,733

world's largest
home in an
airliner 727
BOEING

Bruce Campbell's home is not that large, but it is the biggest of its kind. Campbell lives in 1,066 square feet within a grounded 727 Boeing airplane. The airplane no longer has an engine, but Campbell kept the cockpit and its original instruments. He also installed a transparent floor to make the structure of the plane visible. The retired engineer purchased the plane for $100,000 and paid for its transportation to his property in Oregon. Now trees surround the plane instead of sky. Visitors are welcome to take a tour.

world's largest
house shaped
like a VW beetle
VOGLREITER
RESIDENCE

Architect Markus Voglreiter turned an ordinary home in Gnigl, near Salzburg, Austria, into an attention-grabbing showpiece: a Volkswagen Beetle–shaped house. The eco-friendly home, completed in 2003, is energy efficient and offers separate, comfortable living quarters. The car-shaped extension measures 950 square feet and is over 32 feet tall. At night, two of the home's windows look like car headlights.

world's most
expensive hotel
EMPATHY SUITE, PALMS CASINO,
Las Vegas

A new contender for the world's most expensive hotel emerged in 2019—the Empathy Suite at the Palms Casino Resort in Las Vegas, Nevada. The spectacular space spans 9,000 square feet over two floors and has six works of art by celebrated British artist Damien Hirst. Ever wanted to see a shark suspended in formaldehyde? Well, the Empathy Suite has got it! Hirst also designed the suite; his trademark dots line the columns on the poolside terrace overlooking Las Vegas, while colorful butterfly motifs are set within the marble flooring. And the price? A two-night stay will set you back a cool $200,000.

world's first
hotel made of salt
PALACIO DE SAL

Hotel Palacio de Sal in Uyuni, Bolivia, is the first hotel in the world made completely out of salt. Originally built in 1998, construction began on the new Palacio de Sal in 2004. The hotel overlooks the biggest salt flat in the world, Salar de Uyuni, which covers 4,086 square miles. Builders used around one million blocks of salt to create the hotel walls, floors, ceilings, and furniture. Some of the hotel's thirty rooms have igloo-shaped roofs. The salt flats lie in an area once covered by Lago Minchin, an ancient salt lake. When the lake dried up, it left salt pans, one of which was the Salar de Uyuni.

ANOTHER STRANGE PLACE TO STAY

Hotel shaped like a dog: Dog Bark Park Inn in Cottonwood, Idaho, where you can sleep inside a wooden beagle that measures 33 feet tall and 16 feet wide.

DUBAI'S BURJ KHALIFA WORLD RECORDS:
Tallest building: 2,717 feet
Most floors: 160
Fastest elevators: 55 feet per second

Laid end to end, the steel used here would stretch one-quarter of the way around the world!

EMAAR

world's tallest

building

BURJ

KHALIFA

IT CAN SWAY UP TO 3.9 FEET!

GOING UP!

THE UPPER SECTION IS STEEL FRAMED, SO IT'S POSSIBLE TO MAKE IT TALLER. DURING BUILDING, ITS HEIGHT WAS RAISED THREE TIMES.

world's largest
freestanding building
NEW CENTURY GLOBAL CENTER

The New Century Global Center in Chengdu, southwestern China, is an enormous 18.9 million square feet. That's nearly three times the size of the Pentagon, in Arlington, Virginia. Completed in 2013, the structure is 328 feet tall; 1,640 feet long; and 1,312 feet deep. The multiuse building houses a 4.3-million-square-foot shopping mall, two hotels, an Olympic-size ice rink, a fourteen-screen IMAX cinema complex, and offices. It even has its own Paradise Island, a beach resort complete with artificial sun.

world's largest
swimming pool
CITYSTARS POOL

The Citystars lagoon in Sharm el-Sheikh, Egypt, stretches over 30 acres. It was created by Crystal Lagoons, the same company that built the former record holder at San Alfonso del Mar in Chile. The lagoon at Sharm el-Sheikh cost $5.5 million to create and is designed to be sustainable, using salt water from local underground aquifers. The creators purify this water not just for recreation but also to provide clean, fresh water to the surrounding community.

LARGEST SWIMMING POOLS
Size in acres

Citystars, Sharm el-Sheikh, Egypt: 30

San Alfonso del Mar, Algarrobo, Chile: 19.7

Seagaia Ocean Dome, Miyazaki, Japan (closed): 7.4

Dead Sea, Yuncheng, China: 7.4

Orthlieb Pool, Casablanca, Morocco: 3.7

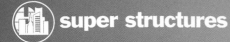

world's longest bridge

DANYANG-KUNSHAN

GRAND BRIDGE

Crossing the floodplain of China's Yangtze River, a terrain of hills, lakes, flatlands, and rice paddies, the 102-mile-long Danyang-Kunshan Grand Bridge is the longest bridge in the world. It is a viaduct, which means it is built using many short spans rather than one long one. They are raised 328 feet above the ground, on average, and are supported on 2,000 pillars. It's a design that helps the high-speed rail bridge to cross the ever-changing landscape between the Chinese cities of Shanghai and Nanjing. Costing $8.5 billion to construct, the bridge took four years to build using a task force of 10,000 laborers.

world's
greenest city
TAMPA

GREENEST CITIES
Treepedia's GVI rating

Tampa, Florida: 36.1%

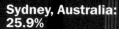

Breda, the Netherlands: 29.3%

Singapore: 29.3%

Sydney, Australia: 25.9%

Vancouver, Canada: 25.9%

According to Treepedia, Tampa, Florida, has the highest percentage of urban greenery in the world. Treepedia is the work of the Senseable City Laboratory at Massachusetts Institute of Technology (MIT). By analyzing panoramas posted on Google Street View, the program assesses the level of vegetation in a city and rates it on a scale of 0–100 in its Green View Index (GVI). It shows the real level of greenery in the streets on which city people live and work. The people behind Treepedia hope to raise greater awareness in cities where trees are lacking and to encourage developers to include them in future projects.

world's largest
vertical garden
KAOHSIUNG CITY

A vertical garden in Kaohsiung City, Taiwan, is the largest in the world at 27,922 square feet, almost the size of ten tennis courts! The garden, also called a "green wall," was completed in June 2015 and forms part of a fence around Cleanaway Company Ltd., a waste-disposal company. Construction took about two months and more than 100,000 plants. From afar, the panorama shows a landscape at sunset, with a bright red sun. However, green walls are not only beautiful; they help to lower pollution and carbon-dioxide emissions.

world's largest
greenhouse
EDEN
PROJECT

COUNTRY WITH THE MOST GREENHOUSES

The Netherlands: Greenhouses cover more than 25 square miles of the country's entire area.

The Eden Project sprawls over 32 acres of land in the countryside of Cornwall, England. Nestled in the cavity of a china clay pit, it's the world's largest greenhouse and has been open since 2003. Eight interlinked, transparent domes house two distinct biomes. The first is a rain forest region and the second is Mediterranean. Each has around one thousand plant varieties. Visitors can see a further three thousand different plants in the 20 acres of outdoor gardens. During construction, the Eden Project used a record-breaking 230 miles of scaffolding.

world's largest tomb of a known individual

QIN SHI HUANG'S TOMB

FIRST EMPEROR OF CHINA

Emperor Qin Shi Huang was the first emperor of a unified China. Before his rule, the territory had been a collection of independent states. He was just forty-nine years old when he died.

QIN SHI HUANG'S TOMB STATS

1974
YEAR OF DISCOVERY

36
NUMBER OF YEARS IT TOOK TO CREATE

8,000
TOTAL NUMBER OF FIGURES FOUND

221–207
DURATION OF THE QIN DYNASTY, BCE

Emperor Qin Shi Huang ruled China from 221 to 207 BCE. In 1974, people digging a well in the fields northeast of Xi'an, in Shaanxi province, accidentally discovered the ancient tomb. Further investigation by archaeologists revealed a burial complex over 20 square miles. A large pit contained 6,000 life-size terra-cotta warrior figures, each one different from the next and dressed according to rank. A second and third pit contained 2,000 more figures; clay horses; about 40,000 bronze weapons; and other artifacts. Historians think that 700,000 people worked for about thirty-six years to create this incredible mausoleum. The emperor's tomb remains sealed to preserve its contents and to protect workers from possible hazards, such as chemical poisoning from mercury in the surrounding soil.

world's largest castle
PRAGUE-CASTLE

Founded in the late ninth century, Prague Castle is officially the largest coherent castle complex in the world. Covering 750,000 square feet, the castle grounds span enough land for seven football fields, with buildings in various architectural styles that have been added and renovated during past centuries. Formerly the home of kings and emperors, the castle is now occupied by the president of the Czech Republic and his family and is also open to tourists. The palace contains four churches, including the famous St. Vitus Cathedral.

world's tallest
sandcastle
BINZ,
Germany

This year's world's tallest sandcastle, measuring an impressive 57 feet 11 inches tall, was completed on June 5, 2019, in the seaside resort of Binz on the island of Ruegen, Germany. Organizer Thomas van Dungen and his team of twelve sculptors and eight technicians worked eight hours a day; it took three-and-a-half weeks to build the sandcastle. The fairy-tale sculpture was constructed for the Sand Sculpture Festival, held annually on the island. It is not the first time this team has attempted to break the world record. In 2017, the group's hopes were shattered when its sandcastle collapsed three days prior to completion.

world's longest
LEGO® ship

WORLD DREAM

In 2018, 1,000 cruise passengers and volunteers came together to help build a replica of the *World Dream* cruise ship, a vessel owned by China's Dream Cruise Management Ltd. Boasting more than 2.5 million LEGO® blocks, this spectacle is the longest LEGO® ship ever built. It's a completely scaled down replica of the *World Dream* cruise ship, with all eighteen of its decks, and measures 27 feet, 8.5 inches in length. On completion it was placed in Hong Kong's terminal for all to see.

world's largest
sculpture cut from a
single piece of stone
SPHINX

The Great Sphinx stands guard near three large pyramids in Giza, Egypt. Historians believe ancient people created the sculpture about 4,500 years ago for the pharaoh Khafre. They carved the sphinx from one mass of limestone in the desert floor, creating a sculpture about 66 feet high and 240 feet long. It has the head of a pharaoh and the body of a lion. The sculpture may represent Ruti, a twin lion god from ancient myths that protected the sun god, Ra, and guarded entrances to the underworld. Sand has covered and preserved the Great Sphinx, but over many years, wind and humidity have worn parts of the soft limestone away, some of which have been restored using blocks of sand and quicklime.

GREAT SPHINX FACTS
Age: 4,500 years (estimated)
Length: 240 feet
Height: 66 feet

TECH

high tech trending

SMILE!
MOST-USED EMOJIS OF 2019
Unicode's list of 2019's top emojis shows that old favorites remain the most used. The crying while laughing emoji and the red heart were the most popular. Various smile emojis, heart eyes, hearts, and kisses also remained near the top, proving that the images continue to be used to show happiness and affection more than any other emotions.

BREATHING EASIER
DEVELOPING 3D RESPIRATORS
The global Covid-19 pandemic of 2019–20 brought a sharp increase in the need for hospital respirators to help patients breathe as the virus attacked their lungs. In early 2020, Spain's Leitat Technology Center produced an emergency breathing device that could be 3D-printed—and therefore mass-produced.

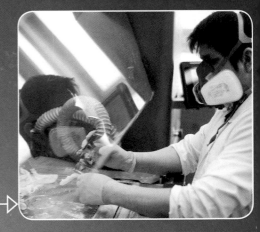

WALKIES!
DRONE: DOG'S BEST FRIEND?
While dog-walking was listed as an approved activity under Covid-19 restrictions in 2020, Cypriot dog-owner Vakis Demetriou proved that he could take the lockdown seriously and still have fun. Attempting to solve the problem of social distancing, he sent a drone to walk his dog for him! He took a video and it went viral across nearly all social media platforms.

BUGHA BUCKS
FORTNITE WORLD CUP WINNER

The first-ever Fortnite world champion was crowned in 2019, with the $3 million prize going to sixteen-year-old Kyle Giersdorf, known as "Bugha." The Pennsylvania native, who is signed to the LA-based e-sports team Sentinels, beat ninety-nine other players in the competition finals. The Fortnite World Cup, which was live streamed to more than two million viewers on YouTube and Twitch, had the largest individual prize in e-sports history.

JENSTAGRAM
QUICKEST TO ONE MILLION

Actress Jennifer Aniston joined Instagram in 2019 and promptly broke the record for reaching one million followers. The fifty-year-old star, who became America's sweetheart with her portrayal of lead character Rachel in the 1994—2004 hit sitcom *Friends*, reached the milestone in just five hours and sixteen minutes, and after ten days her account had an astonishing 16.5 million followers. What was dubbed "The Aniston effect" also led her former *Friends* costars' accounts to get a boost of at least a million new followers each.

celebrity with the most
Instagram followers
CRISTIANO RONALDO

Portuguese soccer icon Cristiano Ronaldo was once again the year's most followed celebrity on Instagram in 2019. He now has 226 million followers, an increase of 69 million over last year. Ronaldo is the forward for Juventus and the captain of the national Portuguese team. His announcement that he was leaving Real Madrid for Juventus is the twentieth most liked Instagram of all time. Other soccer players on the top-ten list for most Instagram followers are Lionel Messi in the no. 8 spot with 156m followers and Neymar in the no. 10 spot with 139m followers.

CELEBRITIES WITH THE MOST INSTAGRAM FOLLOWERS 2019

In millions of followers
(as of June 2020)

- Cristiano Ronaldo: 226
- Ariana Grande: 191
- The Rock: 187
- Kylie Jenner: 182
- Selena Gomez: 181

most retweeted
photo ever
ELLEN
DEGENERES

Ellen DeGeneres's selfie taken at the 2014 Oscars is the most retweeted photo ever. The photo, which pictures DeGeneres, Bradley Cooper, Jennifer Lawrence, and many other celebrities, has over 3.3 million retweets. In just over one hour, the post was retweeted more than one million times. The rush of activity on Twitter crashed the social networking site for a short time. Before the Oscar selfie took over Twitter, President Obama held the record for the most retweeted photo. On November 6, 2012, the president posted an election victory photo and tweet that has been retweeted over 900,000 times.

top-grossing
iPhone gaming apps
ROBLOX
AND CANDY
CRUSH SAGA

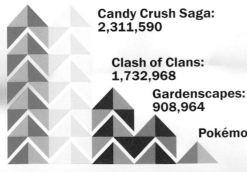

TOP-GROSSING iPHONE GAMING APPS
Daily revenue in U.S. dollars (as of March 2020)

Roblox: 2,311,590

Candy Crush Saga: 2,311,590

Clash of Clans: 1,732,968

Gardenscapes: 908,964

Pokémon GO: 803,849

The free online app Roblox soared from fifth place in 2019 to rank joint first with Candy Crush Saga as the highest daily revenue of all iPhone gaming apps in 2020. Estimates suggest both games generate more than $2.3 million a day. Roblox (pictured) promises a portal to millions of 3D worlds, where an avatar you create and dress can race a car, ride a roller coaster, put on a fashion show, or even slay a dragon. Community members build worlds, which means you can either play someone else's game or build your own. The game is free to download, but upgrades and accessories are available for a fee.

most-viewed
YouTube video ever
"DESPACITO"

Despacito ft. Daddy Yankee

In 2017, "Despacito"
by Luis Fonsi and
Daddy Yankee (later remixed
featuring Justin Bieber) became
the world's most-viewed YouTube
video ever. With more than six billion views and counting,
the video broke the record on the three-billion mark in
August 2017. The record knocked Wiz Khalifa and Charlie
Puth's "See You Again" from the top spot. "See You Again"
had only just taken the crown from Psy's "Gangnam Style."

most-used
Instagram
hashtag

The most popular hashtag on Instagram in 2019 was used to caption a variety of photographs—romantic selfies, cute animals, even shots of new shoes. The picture-sharing platform displays 1.6 billion posts that use the tag #love.

Taking second spot on the listings in 2019 with 988 million posts was #instagood, for photos that are just "too good" not to share. Also rising in the ranks are #photooftheday, #fashion, #beauty, and #happy.

#L😍VE

most-signed
change.org
petition

Justice for
GEORGE FLOYD

In June 2020, "Justice for George Floyd" became change.org's most-signed petition ever, with eighteen million signatures. The petition called for the four police officers involved in Floyd's death to be fired and arrested. George Floyd, a Black man, died on May 25 after white officer Derek Chauvin knelt on his neck for almost nine minutes during an arrest, with three fellow officers standing by. Video footage of the event went viral, sparking anti-racism protests across the globe. Each officer faced charges— Chauvin for second-degree murder and second-degree manslaughter.

most popular

food tech startup
IMPOSSIBLE
BURGER

Technology even drives what we eat these days! The Impossible Burger, created in California's Silicon Valley by a professor of biochemistry, became the no. 1 grocery store item sold in 2019. The plant-based engineered food debuted on grocery shelves in September 2019 and immediately became a favorite. Known to taste like meat, it's entirely made of plants, making it suitable for vegans. The burger was already known to consumers thanks to its earlier appearance in 17,000 restaurants across the country. It is available in supermarket chains such as Gelson's, Wegmans, and Fairway—often outselling everything else in the meat department. Gelson's had to impose a ten-pack limit on the item. In April, Burger King debuted the Impossible Whopper, and by August it was in such demand that they rolled it out nationwide.

Facebook "likes"

CRISTIANO RONALDO

Soccer pro Cristiano Ronaldo retained the top spot on Facebook in 2019 with over 122 million fans. Born in 1985, Ronaldo plays for both the Portuguese national team and the Italian team Juventus. As a teenager, Ronaldo's soccer skills were so impressive that British team Manchester United signed him for around $17 million. In 2008, Ronaldo earned the honor of FIFA World Player of the Year, and in 2017 he won the Ballon d'Or (Golden Ball) award for the fifth time.

PEOPLE WITH THE MOST FACEBOOK FANS

In millions of fans, as of February 2020

Cristiano Ronaldo: 122.46

Shakira: 100.2

Vin Diesel: 96.82

Lionel Messi: 90.28

Eminem: 86.57

Instagram followers
JIFFPOM

On May 3, 2017, and with 4.8 million followers, Jiffpom broke the Guinness World Record for being the most popular dog on Instagram. Three years later, in May 2020, the dog's follower count had passed the ten-million mark. Jiffpom's owner posts snapshots of the fluffy little dog dressed in cute outfits and Jiffpom even has a website. The Pomeranian from the United States has other records to boast of, too. At one time, he held the record for the fastest dog to cover a distance of 16.4 feet on his front legs (7.76 seconds). Another time, he was the record holder for covering 32.8 feet on his hind legs (6.56 seconds).

cat with the most
Instagram followers
NALA CAT

With a total of 4.3 million followers, Nala Cat topped the bill as Instagram's most popular cat in 2019. This figure also saw the popular feline break the Guinness World Record in January 2020, for the cat with the most followers on Instagram. Adopted from a shelter at just five months old, the Siamese-Tabby charms online viewers around the world with her bright blue eyes and supercute headgear.

bestselling
video game ever

T
E
T
R
I
S

Tetris, developed by Russian computer scientist Alexey Pajitnov in 1984, has sold over 500 million copies worldwide—more than any other game. It has been available on almost every video game console since its creation and has seen a resurgence in sales as an app for cell phones and tablets. The iconic puzzle game was the first video game to be exported from the Soviet Union to the United States, the first to be played in outer space, and is often listed as one of the best video games of all time. In 2019, Nintendo released *Tetris* 99 for Nintendo Switch—a multiplayer version of the game that sees ninety-nine players compete online.

CARGANDO

FORTNITE BATTLE ROYALE

Fortnite Battle Royale was the most popular online game in 2019, with almost five million concurrent players. Epic Games developed and published Fortnite Battle Royale, and it is available on PC, PS4, Xbox One, Nintendo Switch, iOS, and Android. The game moved from being the fifth-most-popular online game last year into the top spot this year. The strategic combat game is played by one hundred people at a time. You can play solo or as part of a duo or a group of four against other players. Along the way, you are tasked with finding or creating your own weapons and equipment.

MOST POPULAR ONLINE GAMES
1. *Fortnite Battle Royale*
2. *Playerunknown's Battlegrounds* (PUBG)
3. *League of Legends* (LOL)
4. *Splatoon 2*
5. *Hearthstone*

bestselling
games console
of 2019
NINTENDO
SWITCH

The Nintendo Switch is the best-selling hardware platform again this year (38 million units sold), beating out Sony's PlayStation 4 (13.5 million sold). Nintendo's home console reigned supreme in the U.S. market, with six of the twenty bestselling games of the year being exclusive to the Switch. Within six weeks of launching in March 2020, *Animal Crossing: New Horizons* recorded 13.4 million copies sold, making it the Nintendo Switch's fastest-selling title ever.

bestselling
video game
franchise
of all time
MARIO

Nintendo's Mario franchise has sold 601 million units since the first game was released in 1981. Since then, Mario, his brother Luigi, and other characters like Princess Peach and Yoshi have become household names, starring in a number of games across consoles. In the early games, like *Super Mario World*, players jump over obstacles, collect tokens, and capture flags as Mario journeys through the Mushroom Kingdom to save the princess. The franchise has since diversified to include other popular games, such as *Mario Kart*, a racing game showcasing the inhabitants and landscapes of Mushroom Kingdom.

BESTSELLING VIDEO GAME FRANCHISES
Units sold in millions

 Mario (Nintendo): 601

Pokémon (Game Freak): 340

Grand Theft Auto (Rockstar North): 290

Call of Duty (Infinity Ward): 288

FIFA Soccer: 260

12,140

NUMBER OF PEOPLE ATTENDING
MINEFAIRE: 12,140

150,000

TOTAL AREA, IN SQUARE FEET,
OF *MINECRAFT*-CENTERED
ATTRACTIONS: 150,000

3

NUMBER OF GUINNESS WORLD
RECORDS BROKEN AT THE FAIR: 3

CRAFT

According to Guinness World Records, Minefaire 2016, a gathering of *Minecraft* fans, was the biggest convention ever for a single video game. Held October 15–16, at the Greater Philadelphia Expo Center in Oaks, Pennsylvania, the event attracted 12,140 people. Game developer Markus Persson created *Minecraft* in 2009 and sold it to Microsoft in 2014 for $2.5 billion. Gamers can play alone or with other players online. The game involves breaking and placing blocks to build whatever gamers can imagine—from simple constructions to huge virtual worlds. Attendance was not the only element of Minefaire to gain world-record status. On October 15 the largest-ever *Minecraft* architecture lesson attracted 342 attendees, and American gamer Lestat Wade broke the record for building the tallest staircase in *Minecraft* in one minute.

most popular
beauty and style vlogger
YUYA

The Mexican vlogger Mariand Castrejón Castañeda, aka Yuya, ranks as YouTube's most popular beauty vlogger based on channel subscriptions. Yuya now has more than twenty-four million subscribers. According to Social Blade—YouTube's stats website—Yuya can make up to $372,000 a year from her videos. The young woman started her channel in 2009 after winning a makeup video contest. Since that time, she has posted numerous videos on women's beauty and has released her own line of makeup.

TOP BEAUTY AND STYLE VLOGGERS 2018
Subscribers in millions (as of March 2020)

Yuya: 24.1

Jeffree Star: 16.7

Wengie: 14

Musas: 13.7

NikkieTutorials: 12.3

world's smallest
surgical robot
VERSIUS

British robot specialists Cambridge Medical Robotics developed the world's smallest surgical robot in 2017. Operated by a surgeon using a console guide with a 3-D screen, the robot is able to carry out keyhole surgery. The scientists modeled the robot, called Versius, on the human arm, giving it similar wrist joints to allow maximum flexibility. Keyhole surgery involves making very small cuts on the surface of a person's body, through which a surgeon can operate. The recovery time of the patient is usually quicker when operated on in this way.

OPPORTUNITY

rover on mars

In 2003, NASA sent two rovers to explore planet Mars: *Opportunity* and *Spirit*. The 384-pound *Spirit* rover left Earth in June 2003, to travel 283 million miles to Mars. Its twin *Opportunity* left in July. Equipped with cameras and scientific equipment, the rovers landed on opposite sides of the Red Planet and collected data on its surface. NASA expected the mission to last ninety days but decided to leave the rovers exploring further. NASA lost contact with *Spirit* in 2011 and *Opportunity* in 2018. Only then did NASA declare the mission ended.

LARGE HADRON COLLIDER

largest **single machine**

The Large Hadron Collider (LHC) is a 16-mile, ring-shaped machine that sits 328 feet below ground on the French-Swiss border. In 2008, the European Organization for Nuclear Research (CERN) switched on the machine that thousands of scientists and engineers spent years building. They hope that the gigantic collider will explain many mysteries of the universe by examining some of its tiniest particles, called hadrons. The machine makes these particles travel almost at the speed of light and records what happens when they collide. The aim is to examine various scientific theories, including the idea that the universe originated in a massive cosmic explosion known as the Big Bang.

Fanny is a massive 26-foot-high, 51-foot-long, fire-breathing dragon. She is also the world's biggest walking robot. In 2012, a German company designed and built Fanny using both hydraulic and electronic parts. She is radio remote-controlled with nine controllers, while 238 sensors allow the robot to assess her environment. She does this while walking on her four legs or stretching wings that span 39 feet. Powered by a 140-horsepower diesel engine, Fanny weighs a hefty 24,250 pounds—as much as two elephants—and breathes real fire using 24 pounds of liquid gas.

biggest
walking robot
FANNY

FANNY STATS:

09/27/2012
DATE OF FANNY'S LAUNCH

26′ 10″
FANNY'S HEIGHT: in feet and inches

51′ 6″
FANNY'S LENGTH: in feet and inches

12′
FANNY'S BODY WIDTH: in feet

39′
FANNY'S WINGSPAN: in feet

Covid-19
trending

WRITTEN ON THE WALLS
COVID-19 STREET ART

For many leaving their houses during the Covid-19 lockdown, the world looked very different. During the crisis, street artists expressed their fears, hopes, and solidarity with others through new pandemic-themed artworks in their cities. These works ranged from grateful murals depicting doctors and nurses as superheroes—such as the one painted by the street artist FAKE in Amsterdam—to ironic but bold warnings for people to stay inside and stay safe.

THE TEN-DAY HOSPITAL
CONSTRUCTION LIVE STREAMED

The spread of Covid-19 massively overwhelmed health-care systems in many countries. In Wuhan, China, where the virus was first detected, the country's government responded by building two entirely new hospitals at amazing speeds. Huoshenshan Hospital, with 1,000 new beds, took just ten days to build, and its construction was live streamed around the world as proof of what hard work and cooperation can achieve.

SONGS OF SURVIVAL
ITALY'S SPIRIT STAYS STRONG
One of the earliest European countries to be hit by the pandemic, Italy was closely watched when it entered lockdown. The nation's community spirit became evident when videos started appearing online, showing people on their balconies singing rousing songs and playing music to keep up their morale. Heartwarming videos showed neighborhoods coming together on balconies and at windows to applaud the impromptu performers.

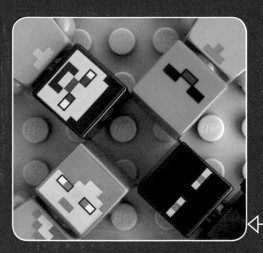

CLASS OF 2020
GRADUATION MOVES ONLINE
Students around the world had their education disrupted during the crisis, forcing educators to devise ways to teach and communicate remotely. In Japan, a group of elementary and middle schoolers reconstructed their physically canceled graduation ceremony via the video game *Minecraft*, building an assembly hall and stage and gathering there virtually.

WASH YOUR HANDS
VIRAL DANCE CRAZE
Handwashing memes were everywhere during the Covid-19 crisis, as governments advised citizens to wash their hands thoroughly and frequently to help prevent the virus from spreading. In Vietnam, the National Institute of Occupational Safety and Health even joined with singer Khac Hun to make a song encouraging citizens to wash hands properly. The video took off on TikTok to become a viral dance challenge.

6

amazing ANIMALS

amazing animals
trending

SAFE AND SOUND
ESCAPING THE BUSHFIRES

While images of the record season of Australian bushfires in 2019 horrified people around the world, one heartwarming side to the disaster emerged. Photographs of wild animals being rescued—from injured koalas cuddling soft toys to baby kangaroos in firefighters' arms—stirred hearts worldwide. Australia has dedicated organizations for wildlife rescue volunteers to help evacuate animals from affected areas.

SOCCER HEAD
UNDERWATER PHOTOGRAPH OF THE YEAR

Italian underwater photographer Pasquale Vassallo called his winning photo *Octopus Training*. At first, Pasquale only spotted the soccer ball floating on the water, but closer inspection revealed it was accompanied by an octopus. Perhaps the creature was intrigued by the way the ball floated on the water and decided to join it for a while as it bobbed along on the current.

RARE BEAR
ALBINO GIANT PANDA

A rare albino giant panda made headlines in 2019 after being spotted roaming China's Wolong Nature Reserve. Infrared shots taken of the all-white creature mark its first time caught on camera, and the photos have thrilled panda experts, who know albinism is possible in the species but had never seen an occurrence. Experts say the rare bear was probably one to two years old and appeared healthy.

OLD MAN OF THE ISLAND
WORLD'S OLDEST-KNOWN LAND ANIMAL

A tortoise became the world's oldest-known land animal in 2019. "Jonathan" the tortoise was probably born in 1832 and has lived at the governor's residence on the island of St. Helena since 1882. At 187 years, Jonathan has far outlived giant tortoises' 150-year life expectancy. Despite being blind and lacking a sense of smell, he is still good-tempered and has good hearing.

PIG SMART
FIRST RECORD OF PIGS USING TOOLS

A visiting researcher at a Paris zoo made a startling discovery: The Visayan warty pigs there were using tools— an important marker of advanced cognitive abilities. Pigs were seen using a piece of bark in their mouths to dig in the soil to build nests. Although pigs are known to be intelligent, this is the first time scientists have seen that they are capable of the thinking required to use tools.

world's sleepiest animal KOALA

Australia's koala sleeps for up to twenty hours a day and still manages to look sleepy when awake. This is due to the koala's unbelievably monotonous diet. It feeds, mostly at night, on the aromatic leaves of eucalyptus trees. The leaves have little nutritional or calorific value, so the marsupial saves energy by snoozing. It jams its rear end into a fork in the branches of its favorite tree so it cannot fall out while snoozing.

world's
best glider

Flying squirrels are champion animal gliders. The Japanese giant flying squirrel has been scientifically recorded making flights of up to 164 feet from tree to tree. These creatures have been estimated to make 656-foot flights when flying downhill. The squirrel remains aloft using a special flap of skin on either side of its body, which stretches between wrist and ankle. Its fluffy tail acts as a stabilizer to keep it steady, and the squirrel changes direction by twisting its wrists and moving its limbs.

FLYING
SQUIRREL

WORLD'S GLIDERS
Distance in feet

Colugo, or flying lemur: 230

Draco, or flying lizard: 197

Flying squid: 164

Flying squirrel: 656

Flying fish: 655

AFRICAN BUSH ELEPHANT

world's heaviest land mammal

The African bush elephant is the world's largest living land animal. The biggest known bush elephant stood 13.8 feet at the shoulder and had an estimated weight of 13.5 tons. It is also the animal with the largest outer ears. The outsize flappers help keep the animal cool on the open savanna. The Asian elephant has much smaller earflaps, because it lives in the forest and is not exposed to the same high temperatures.

world's
tiniest bat
KITTI'S HOG-NOSED BAT

This little critter, the Kitti's hog-nosed bat, is just 1.3 inches long, with a wingspan of 6.7 inches, and weighs 0.07–0.10 ounces. It's tied for first place as world's smallest mammal with Savi's pygmy shrew, which is longer at 2.1 inches but lighter at 0.04–0.06 ounces. The bat lives in west central Thailand and southeast Myanmar, and the shrew is found from the Mediterranean to Southeast Asia.

world's largest
primate
GORILLA

The largest living primates are the eastern gorillas, and the biggest subspecies is the very rare mountain gorilla. The tallest known was an adult male silverback, named for the color of the fur on his back. He stood at 6.4 feet tall, but he was an exception—silverbacks generally grow no bigger than 5.9 feet tall. Gorillas have long arms: The record holder had an arm span measuring 8.9 feet, while adult male humans have an average arm span of just 5.9 feet.

world's most
colorful monkey
MANDRILL

The male mandrill's face is as flamboyant as his rear end. The vivid colors of both are brightest at breeding time. The colors announce to his rivals that he is an alpha male and he has the right to breed with the females. His exceptionally long and fang-like canine teeth reinforce his dominance. The mandrill is the world's largest monkey, as well as the most colorful.

CHEETAH

world's fastest land animal

The fastest reliably recorded running speed of any animal was that of a zoo-bred cheetah that reached an incredible 61 miles per hour on a flat surface. The record was achieved in 2012, from a standing start by a captive cheetah at Cincinnati Zoo. More recently, wild cheetahs have been timed while actually hunting their prey in the bush in Botswana. Using GPS technology and special tracking collars, the scientists found that these cheetahs had a top speed of 58 miles per hour over rough terrain.

FASTEST LAND ANIMALS
Speed in miles per hour

Lion: 30

Springbok: 55

Pronghorn: 55

Ostrich: 60

Cheetah: 65

animal

PARATARSOTOMUS MACROPALPIS

Step aside, cheetah! A tiny mite, just 0.028 inches long but with the ginormous name *Paratarsotomus macropalpis*, has set a new record for the fastest-running terrestrial animal ever, according to Stanford University. The mite can run twenty times faster than a cheetah, size for size, and can even outrun the previous record holder—the Australian tiger beetle. While the beetle can whiz along at 171 body lengths per second and the cheetah 16 body lengths per second, the mite achieves an astonishing 322 body lengths per second at top speed. That's the equivalent of Usain Bolt racing at 1,400 miles per hour!

world's largest
big cat

TIGER

There are only five big cats: tiger, lion, jaguar, leopard, and snow leopard. The biggest and heaviest is the Siberian, or Amur, tiger, which lives in the taiga (boreal forest) of eastern Siberia, where it hunts deer and wild boar. The largest reliably measured tigers have been about 11.8 feet long and weighed 705 pounds, but there have been claims for larger individuals, such as the male shot in the Sikhote-Alin Mountains in 1950. That tiger weighed 847 pounds.

world's noisiest
land animal
HOWLER MONKEY

The howler monkeys of Latin America are deafening. Males have an especially large hyoid bone. This horseshoe-shaped bone in the neck creates a chamber that makes the monkey's deep guttural growls sound louder for longer.

It is said that their calls can be heard up to 3 miles away. Both males and females call, and they holler mainly in the morning. It is thought that these calls are often one troop telling neighboring troops where they are.

137

Giraffes living on the savannas of eastern and southern Africa are the world's tallest animals. The tallest known bull giraffe measured 19 feet from the ground to the top of his horns. He could have looked over the top of a London double-decker bus or peered into the upstairs window of a two-story house. Despite having considerably longer necks than we do, giraffes have the same number of neck vertebrae. They also have long legs with which they can either speedily escape from predators or kick them to keep them away.

GIRAFFE STATS

6
HEIGHT OF A CALF AT BIRTH (in feet)

25
AVERAGE LIFE SPAN (in years)

100
ADULT'S DAILY FOOD CONSUMPTION
(in pounds of leaves and twigs)

GIRAFFE

living animal

world's tallest

REACHING GREAT HEIGHTS

A giraffe's tongue can grow up to 21 inches in length. This helps the animal reach leaves on the topmost branches of a tree when it is looking for food.

world's longest tooth
NARWHAL

The narwhal's "sword" is an enormously elongated spiral tooth, or tusk. In male narwhals it can grow to more than 8.2 feet long. Only about 15 percent of females grow a tusk, which typically is smaller than a male tusk, with a less noticeable spiral. It has been suggested that the tusk serves as an adornment to attract the opposite sex—the larger a male narwhal's tusk, the more attractive he is to females. It is also thought to be a sensory organ that detects changes in the seawater, such as saltiness, which could help the narwhal find food. Observers have also noted that the narwhal uses its tusk to stun prey.

the world's largest
living animal
BLUE
WHALE

Blue whales are truly colossal. The largest one accurately measured was 110 feet long, and the heaviest weighed 209 tons. They feed on tiny krill, which they filter from the sea. On land, the largest known animal was a Titanosaur—a huge dinosaur that lived in what is now Argentina 101 million years ago. A skeleton found in 2014 suggests the creature was 121 feet long and weighed 77 tons. It belongs to a young Titanosaur, so an adult may have been bigger than a blue whale.

world's biggest fish
WHALE SHARK

Recognizable from its spotted skin and enormous size, the whale shark is the world's largest living fish. It grows to a maximum length of about 66 feet. Like the blue whale, this fish feeds on some of the smallest creatures: krill, marine larvae, small fish, and fish eggs. The whale shark is also a great traveler: One female was tracked swimming 4,800 miles from Mexico—where hundreds of whale sharks gather each summer to feed—to the middle of the South Atlantic Ocean, where it is thought she may have given birth.

the shark most dangerous to people
GREAT WHITE SHARK

SHARK ATTACKS
Number of humans attacked

Great white: 326

Tiger shark: 129

Bull shark: 116

Sand tiger shark: 41

The great white shark is at the top of the list for the highest number of attacks on people. The largest reliably measured fish was 21 feet long, making it the largest predatory fish in the sea. Its jaws are lined with large, triangular, serrated teeth that can slice through flesh, sinew, and even bone. However, there were just sixty-four reported nonprovoked attacks by sharks of any kind in 2019, and only two of those proved fatal. Humans are not this creature's top food of choice. People don't have enough fat on their bodies. Mature white sharks prefer blubber-rich seals, dolphins, and whales. It is likely that many of the attacks on people are probably cases of mistaken identity.

world's largest
invertebrate
COLOSSAL SQUID

The colossal squid is a true monster of the deep. Its body can reach 9 feet long with large tail fins, and it can weigh up to 1,000 pounds. A colossal squid's eyes are the size of soccer balls and are the biggest in the animal kingdom. The club-like ends of its two long, retractable tentacles have two rows of swiveling hooks, as well as suckers with hard, toothed rims. There are also hooks and suckers on the eight shorter arms, making the squid a formidable predator. Its main prey is thought to be Patagonian toothfish, which the squid grabs with its tentacles and grasps with its arms while chopping it to pieces using its sharp parrotlike beak.

The reticulated python of Indonesia is the world's longest snake. One, called Fragrant Flower, counts among the longest pythons ever discovered. It was living in the wilds of Java until villagers captured it. A local government official confirmed it was 48.8 feet long and weighed 985 pounds. These creatures are constricting snakes: They squeeze the life out of their prey before consuming. In 1999, a 22.9-foot-long python swallowed a sun bear in Balikpapan, East Kalimantan.

world's longest snake
PYTHON

world's
**largest
lizard**

KOMODO DRAGON

There are dragons on Indonesia's Komodo Island, and they're dangerous. The Komodo dragon's jaws are lined with sixty replaceable, serrated, backward-pointing teeth. Its saliva is laced with **deadly** bacteria and venom that the dragon works into a wound, ensuring its prey will die quickly. Prey can be as big as a pig or deer, because this lizard is the world's largest. It can grow up to 10.3 feet long and weigh 366 pounds.

deadliest frog

POISON
DART FROG

A poison dart frog's skin exudes toxins. There are several species, and the more vivid a frog's color, the more deadly its poison. The skin color warns potential predators that the frogs are not good to eat, although one snake is immune to the chemicals and happily feeds on these creatures. It is thought that the frogs do not manufacture their own poisons, but obtain the chemicals from their diet of ants, millipedes, and mites. The most deadly species to people is also the largest, Colombia's golden poison dart frog. At just one inch long, a single frog has enough poison to kill ten to twenty people.

world's largest
reptile
SALTWATER
CROCODILE

The saltwater crocodile, or "saltie," is the world's largest living reptile. Males can grow to over 20 feet long, but a few old-timers become real monsters. A well-known crocodile in the Segama River, Borneo, left an impression on a sandbank that measured 33 feet. The saltie can be found in areas from eastern India to northeast Australia, where it lives in mangroves, estuaries, and rivers. It is sometimes found out at sea. The saltie is an ambush predator, grabbing any animal that enters its domain—including people. Saltwater crocodiles account for twenty to thirty attacks on people per year, up to half of which are fatal.

"SALTIE" crocodiles can live for up to 70 years in the wild.

world's smallest owl
NORTH AMERICAN ELF OWL

The North American elf owl is one of three tiny owls vying for this title. It is about 5 inches long and weighs 1.5 ounces. This owl spends winter in Mexico and flies to nest in Arizona and New Mexico in spring. It often occupies cavities excavated by woodpeckers in saguaro cacti. Rivals for the title of smallest owl are Peru's long-whiskered owlet and Mexico's Tamaulipas pygmy owl, which are both a touch shorter but slightly heavier, making the elf owl the smallest of all.

FIVE OF THE WORLD'S OWLS
Height in inches

North American elf owl: 5   **Little owl: 8.7**   **Barn owl: 15**   **Snowy owl: 28**   **Great gray owl: 33**

world's smelliest bird
HOATZIN

The hoatzin eats leaves, flowers, and fruit, and ferments the food in its crop (a pouch in its esophagus). This habit leaves the bird with a foul odor, which has led people to nickname the hoatzin the "stinkbird." About the size of a pheasant, this bird lives in the Amazon and Orinoco river basins of South America. A hoatzin chick has sharp claws on its wings, like a pterodactyl. If threatened by a snake, the chick jumps from the nest into the water, then uses its wing claws to help it climb back up.

bird with the
longest tail
RIBBON-
TAILED
ASTRAPIA

The ribbon-tailed astrapia has the longest feathers in relation to body size of any wild bird. The male, which has a beautiful, iridescent blue-green head, sports a pair of white ribbon-shaped tail feathers that are more than 3.3 feet long—three times the length of its 13-inch-long body. It is one of Papua New Guinea's birds of paradise and lives in the mountain forests of central New Guinea, where males sometimes have to untangle their tails from the foliage before they can fly.

bird with the longest wingspan
WANDERING ALBATROSS

Long, narrow wings, like those of a glider aircraft, are the mark of the wandering albatross. The longest authenticated measurement for wingspan was taken in 1965 from an old-timer, its pure white plumage an indication of its age. Its wingspan was 11.9 feet. This seabird rarely flaps its wings but uses the wind and updrafts from waves to soar effortlessly over the ocean.

BIRDS WITH LONG WINGSPANS
Wingspan in feet

Wandering albatross: 11.9

Great white pelican: 11.81

Andean condor: 10.5

Marabou stork: 10.5

Southern royal albatross: 9.8

world's loudest bird
AMAZON WHITE BELLBIRD

The Amazon white bellbird calls three times louder than its nearest rival (the aptly named screaming piha) for the title of world's loudest bird. The male's deafening song has decibel levels equal to the loudest musical instruments. As it sings, the bird swivels dramatically, and in the song's final flourish the sound is directed at a watching female. Scientists have discovered that the louder the songs, the shorter they are. The dove-sized birds probably have only so much puff to generate these exceptionally loud songs, but they do have well-developed abdominal muscles and ribs in order to kick up the loudest ruckus in the avian world.

bird that builds
largest nest
BALD EAGLE

With a wingspan over 6.6 feet, bald eagles need space to land and take off—so their nests can be gargantuan. Over the years, a nest built by a pair of bald eagles in St. Petersburg, Florida, has taken on epic proportions. Measuring 9.5 feet across and 20 feet deep, it is made of sticks, grass, and moss. At one stage it was thought to have weighed at least 2 tons, making it the largest nest ever constructed by a pair of birds. Although one pair nests at a time, these huge structures are often the work of several pairs of birds, each building on top of the work of their predecessors.

THE WORLD'S LARGEST NESTS
Diameter in inches

Bald eagle: 114   Golden eagle: 55   White stork: 57

5.9 in

4.5 in

world's
largest bird egg
AFRICAN OSTRICH EGG

The ostrich lays the largest eggs of any living bird, yet they are the smallest eggs relative to the size of the mother's body. Each egg is some 5.9 inches long and weighs about 3.5–5 pounds, while the mother is about 6.2 feet tall and the male is about 7.8 feet tall, making the ostrich the world's largest living bird. The female lays about fifty eggs per year, and each egg contains as much yolk and albumen as twenty-four hens' eggs. It takes an hour to soft boil an ostrich egg!

EMPEROR PENGUIN STATS

80
AVERAGE WEIGHT OF AN ADULT:
80 pounds

1,640
DEPTHS AN ADULT CAN SWIM TO:
1,640 feet

22
LENGTH OF TIME UNDERWATER:
Up to 22 minutes

FIVE OF THE WORLD'S PENGUINS
Height in inches

Emperor: 48   **King: 39**   **Gentoo: 35**   **Macaroni: 28**   **Galápagos: 19**

world's biggest
penguin

EMPEROR PENGUIN

At 4 feet tall, the emperor penguin is the world's biggest living penguin. It has a most curious lifestyle, breeding during the long, dark Antarctic winter. The female lays a single egg and carefully passes it to the male. She then heads out to sea to feed, while he remains with the egg balanced on his feet and tucked under a fold of blubber-rich skin. There he stands with all the other penguin dads, huddled together to keep warm in the blizzards and 100-mile-per-hour winds that scour the icy continent. Come spring, the egg hatches, the female returns, and Mom and Dad swap duties, taking turns to feed and care for their fluffy chick.

world's longest
insect migration

GLOBE SKIMMER

Each year millions of dragonflies fly thousands of miles across the Indian Ocean from Southern India to East Africa. Most of them are globe skimmers, a species known to fly long distances and at altitudes up to 3,280 feet. They can travel 2,175 miles in 24 hours. Coral cays on the way have little open freshwater so the insects stay there for a few days before moving on to East Africa. Here, they follow the rains, at each stop taking advantage of temporary rainwater pools to lay their eggs to hatch where their young can rapidly develop. Four generations are involved in a round trip of about 11,000 miles—farther than the distance from New York to Sydney.

world's fastest
flying insect
DESERT
LOCUST

Flying insects are difficult to clock, and many impressive speeds have been claimed. The fastest airspeed reliably timed was by fifteen desert locusts that managed an average of 21 miles per hour. Airspeed is the actual speed at which the insect flies. It is different from ground speed, which is often enhanced by favorable winds. A black cutworm moth whizzed along at 70 miles per hour while riding the winds ahead of a cold front. The most shocking measurement, however, is that of a horsefly with an estimated airspeed of 90 miles per hour while chasing an air-gun pellet! The speed, understandably, has not been verified.

world's deadliest
animal
MOSQUITO

Female mosquitoes live on the blood
of birds and mammals—humans
included. However, the problem is not
what they take, but what they leave
behind. In some mosquitos' saliva are
organisms that cause the world's most
deadly illnesses, including malaria,
yellow fever, dengue fever, West Nile
virus, and encephalitis. It is estimated
that mosquitoes transmit diseases
to 700 million people every year, of
which 725,000 die. Mosquitoes are the
deadliest family of insects on earth.

world's heaviest spider
GOLIATH BIRD-EATING TARANTULA

FOUR OF THE WORLD'S SPIDERS
Leg span in inches

| Giant huntsman spider: 12 | Goliath bird-eating tarantula: 11 | Brazilian wandering spider: 5.9 | Golden silk orb-weaver: 5 |

The size of a dinner plate, the female goliath bird-eating tarantula has a leg span of 11 inches and weighs up to 6.17 ounces. This is the world's heaviest spider and a real nightmare for an arachnophobe (someone with a fear of spiders). Its fangs can pierce a person's skin, but its venom is no worse than a bee sting. The hairs on its body are more of a hazard. When threatened, it rubs its abdomen with its hind legs and releases tiny hairs that cause severe irritation to the skin. Despite its name, this spider does not actually eat birds very often.

pets
trending

BIG MOO-D
IF COWS COULD TALK
Research from the University of Sydney shows that cows communicate their feelings to each other. Researchers found that "moos" changed depending on a cow's mood: to express excitement or fear, for example. Alexandra Green, who led the study, says that one can tell individual cows from one another by their voices.

HANDSOME BOY!
SHARP DRESSER
Images of the canine "offspring" of actress Sophie Turner and singer Joe Jonas went viral in 2019, and the Internet couldn't handle his cuteness. Porky Basquiat Jonas, an Alaskan Klee Klai, overshadowed everyone at Turner and Jonas's June wedding in his custom tuxedo, and he was captured stealing the show in a group photo of all the suited-and-booted groomsmen.

#FLUFFYCOW
BOVINE BEAUTIES

The big trend in cattle styling is apparently the blow-dry: #FluffyCow began in 2015, but the Internet's appetite for immaculately styled cows has not let up, with plenty of Tumblr posts and listicles dedicated to the best in show. Cows are blow-dried and styled before livestock shows and state fairs, in which owners show off their shiny-haired cattle in attempts to win the top prizes.

CHONKY BOY
BEEJAY FINDS A HOME

A new star was born when the Morris Animal Shelter in Pennsylvania tweeted a picture of BeeJay, a huge 26-pound cat looking for a new home. The domestic shorthair was an immediate hit: The Twittersphere was charmed by BeeJay's "chonky" form. The shelter says it received more than 3,000 applications from people wanting to give BeeJay a home.

RESCUE PUPPY
UNICORN DOG GOES VIRAL

Narwhal the "unicorn puppy" became an Internet sensation in 2019. Narwhal was born with a tail-like appendage on his forehead and was rescued from the streets by Mac's Mission in Missouri. His photo was retweeted nearly 130,000 times in the first week after posting, and this has helped bring attention to disabled rescue dogs at the Mission.

world's fluffiest rabbit
ANGORA RABBIT

In most people's opinion, the Angora rabbit is the world's fluffiest bunny. The breed originated in Turkey and is thought to be one of the world's oldest rabbit breeds as well. It became popular with the French court in the mid-eighteenth century. Today it is bred for its long, soft, wool, which is shorn every three to four months. One of the fluffiest bunnies is buff-colored Franchesca, owned by English Angora rabbit expert Dr. Betty Chu. In 2014, Franchesca's fur was measured at 14.37 inches, making a world record that is yet to be beaten.

world's smallest horse
BOMBEL

Bombel is a miniature Appaloosa living in Poland. At just 22 inches from the bottom of his hooves to the top of his shoulder blades, he is the world's shortest living stallion. According to the American Miniature Horse Association, a "mini-horse" must be less than 38 inches tall at the withers, so Bombel more than qualifies. Bombel gets his name, meaning "Bubble," on account of his plump body and exceedingly short legs. Once a month, he visits children in the local hospital. However, Bombel is not the shortest horse of all time. That was Thumbelina, a sorrel brown mare from St. Louis, Missouri. She measured 17.5 inches at the shoulder.

world's hairiest dog
KOMONDOR

The world's hairiest dog breed is the komondor, or Hungarian sheepdog. It is a powerful dog that was bred originally to guard sheep. Its long, white, dreadlock-like "cords" enable it not only to blend in with the flock but also to protect itself from bad weather and bites from wolves. This is a large dog, standing over 27.5 inches at the shoulders. Its hairs are up to 10.6 inches long, giving it the heaviest coat of any dog.

America's most popular **dog breed**
LABRADOR

AMERICA'S MOST POPULAR DOGS
Rating

1. **Labrador Retriever**
2. **German Shepherd**
3. **Golden Retriever**
4. **French Bulldog**
5. **Bulldog**
6. **Poodle**
7. **Beagle**
8. **Rottweiler**
9. **German Short-haired Pointer**
10. **Pembroke Welsh Corgi**

The Labrador retriever holds the top spot as America's most popular dog breed for a 29th consecutive year. Its eager-to-please temperament makes it an ideal companion. The Labrador was originally bred as a gun dog that fetched game birds shot by hunters. Now, aside from being a family pet, it is a favored assistance dog that helps blind people and a good detection dog used by law-enforcement agencies. A newcomer to the list, the Corgi (pictured) ousts the Yorkshire Terrier to claim spot no. 10.

world's
tallest

living dog
FREDDY

At 40.75 inches tall, a Great Dane named Freddy claimed the title of world's tallest living dog in December 2016 and holds the record to this day. He lives in the United Kingdom with his owner, Claire Stoneman, and his sister, Fleur. According to Claire, her two pets cost her around $1,400 a year in food alone, with Freddy eating 2.2 pounds of ground beef, 10.5 ounces of liver, and 9 ounces of steak a day. When Freddy stands on his hind legs, he towers over his owner at a height of 90 inches.

WORLD'S

Chihuahuas are the world's smallest dog breed—and the smallest of them all is Miracle Milly, a Chihuahua from Puerto Rico. She measures just 3.8 inches tall, no bigger than a sneaker. The shortest is Heaven Sent Brandy from Largo, Florida, just 6 inches from her nose to the tip of her tail. Chihuahuas originated in Mexico and may have predated the Maya. They are probably descendants of the Techichi, an early companion dog of the Toltec civilization (900–1168 CE).

smallest dog

CHIHUAHUA

America's most popular
cat breed
RAGDOLL

According to the Cat Fanciers' Association, the Ragdoll melted the hearts of American cat lovers in 2019. This is the second year running that the "Raggie" has taken top spot as the most-registered cat breed of the year. With its lush, silky fur and big blue eyes, this is a cat that loves to be around human beings, relaxing like a "rag doll" when curled up on your lap. The Exotic Shorthair, with its teddy-bear looks, had to settle for second place in the listings.

AMERICA'S MOST POPULAR CATS
Rating
1. Ragdoll
2. Exotic Shorthair
3. British Shorthair
4. Persian
5. Maine Coon Cat
6. Devon Rex
7. American Shorthair
8. Abyssinian
9. Sphynx
10. Scottish Fold

world's baldest cat

SPHYNX

The sphynx breed of cats is famous for its wrinkles and the lack of a normal coat, but it is not entirely hairless. Its skin is like the softest chamois leather, but it has a thin layer of down. It behaves more like a dog than a cat, greeting owners when they come home, and is friendly to strangers. The breed originated in Canada, where a black-and-white cat gave birth to a hairless kitten called Prune in 1966. Subsequent breeding gave rise to the sphynx.

7

incredible
EARTH

incredible earth
trending

SHARON?
THUNBERG STRIKES BACK

Climate activist Greta Thunberg changed her Twitter bio and name many times throughout 2019 to make light of how powerful people described her—from "kind" but "poorly informed" (Russian President Vladimir Putin), to "a teenager working on her anger management problem" (President Donald Trump). Her funniest change was to "Sharon" in early 2020, after a celebrity on a quiz show was asked to name her and guessed that name instead.

I DO!
VOLCANIC WEDDING GOES VIRAL

Photos of Chino Vaflor and Kat Bautista Palomar's wedding ceremony went viral in 2019, showing them continuing with the event as Taal, the most active volcano in the Philippines, erupted with smoke and ash in the background. The wedding was less than 6.2 miles away from the volcano, which began spewing lava only a day later.

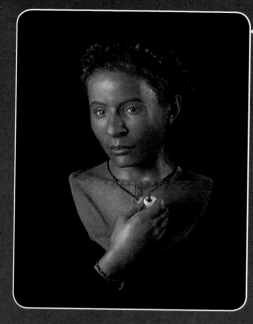

ANCESTORS REBORN
REVIVING ANCIENT PEOPLE

An exhibit at Brighton Museum and Art Gallery, England, brought the region's long-gone ancestors to life in 2019, showcasing realistic reconstructions of people from ancient remains. Using modern forensic technology, scientists worked with artists to create lively, lifelike models of seven individuals—including 5,600-year-old Whitehawk Woman (pictured), who probably died in childbirth, and 4,200-year-old Ditchling Road Man, who likely arrived in Britain from continental Europe.

NOT-SO-GREEN THUMB
PLANT FAUX PAS

Twenty-four-year-old Caelie Wilkes was the first to laugh when she posted pictures to Facebook in 2019 of a perfect succulent plant, which she had been watering for two years—only to discover that it was artificial. She claimed that she realized her mistake when she tried to repot her green pride and joy. People on social media have questioned how it took her so long to notice. Where did all that water go?

ICY ERUPTION
RARE PHENOMENON

A National Weather Service meteorologist's pics went viral in February 2019 after he captured a so-called ice volcano erupting near Lake Michigan. Despite the term, there are no actual volcanoes in the area—just a rare phenomenon in which hollow cones are formed by water trapped beneath an ice sheet building up pressure.

oldest tree on earth
BRISTLECONE PINE

An unnamed bristlecone pine in the White Mountains of California is the world's oldest continually standing tree. It is 5,067 years old, beating its bristlecone rivals the Methuselah (4,861 years old) and Prometheus (4,849 years old). Sweden is home to an even older tree, a Norway spruce (which are often used as Christmas trees) that took root about 9,551 years ago. However, this tree has not been standing continually, but is long-lived because it can clone itself. When the trunk dies, a new one grows up from the same rootstock, so in theory it could live forever.

A coast redwood named Hyperion is the world's tallest known living tree. It is 379.1 feet tall, and could have grown taller if a woodpecker had not hammered its top. It's growing in a remote part of the Redwood National and State Parks in Northern California, but its exact location is kept a secret for fear that too many visitors would upset its ecosystem. It is thought to be 700 to 800 years old.

world's tallest tree
CALIFORNIA REDWOOD

WORLD'S TALLEST TREES
Height in feet

California redwood,
California, USA: 379.1

Mountain ash, Styx
Valley, Tasmania: 327.4

Coast Douglas-fir,
Oregon, USA: 327.3

Sitka spruce,
California, USA: 317

Giant sequoia,
California, USA: 314

largest and heaviest fruit
PUMPKIN

The world's largest-ever fruit was a cultivated pumpkin grown by Swiss gardener Beni Meier, the world's first non-American giant pumpkin champion. His record-breaking squash weighed an incredible 2,324 pounds, and Beni had to hire special transportation to take the fruit for weighing in at the October 2014 European Championship Pumpkin Weigh-Off, held in Germany. The seeds of nearly all giant pumpkins can trace their ancestry back to a species of squash that was cultivated by Canadian pumpkin breeder Howard Dill.

world's toughest leaf

AMAZON WATER LILY

The leaf of the giant Amazon water lily can grow as wide as 8.6 feet across. It has an upturned rim and a waxy, water-repellent upper surface. On the underside of the leaf is a riblike structure that traps air so the leaf floats easily. The ribs are also lined with sharp spines that protect them from aquatic plant eaters. The leaf is so large and so strong that it can support up to ninety-nine pounds in weight.

world's largest
single flower
RAFFLESIA

Conservationists in Indonesia have found the biggest specimen ever of a species already recognized as the world's largest single flower. The giant *Rafflesia tuan-mudae* is a huge fleshy red flower with white spots on its petals. It grows in Southeast Asia. This monster was discovered on the island of Sumatra. At 3 feet 8 inches across, it beats the previous record-holder by 1.6 inches and is the largest of its kind ever documented. A parasite of jungle vines, *Rafflesia* is sometimes known as the "corpse flower" on account of the stench of rotting meat that it produces to attract insects. It lasts for about a week before it withers and rots.

world's most
dangerous
mushroom
DEATH CAP

Don't eat the death cap—the warning is in the name. This fungus is responsible for the most deaths by mushroom poisoning and can be found all over the world, including the United States. The mushroom's toxins damage the liver and kidneys, and it is not possible to destroy the dangerous chemicals by cooking, freezing, or drying. The Roman emperor Claudius is thought to have died from death-cap poisoning in 54 CE. He liked to eat salads of Caesar mushrooms, an almost identical edible species, but was served the killer fungus instead.

VERYOVKINA CAVE STATS

1968
YEAR OF DISCOVERY

7,257
DEPTH DISCOVERED TO DATE
(in feet)

2018
YEAR CURRENT DEPTH
ESTABLISHED

The limestone-rich Western Caucasus region in the Eurasian country of Georgia has some extraordinary cave systems. Among the caverns there is Veryovkina, the deepest cave in the world. It's over 7,257 feet deep! (That's more than sixteen times taller than the Great Pyramid of Giza.) It took as many as thirty expeditions over more than fifty years before Russian cavers reached the record depth, and they suspect there is even more to explore.

EXTRAORDINARY LENGTHS
In order to establish the record-breaking depths of Veryovkina Cave, cavers took three days to get down and three days to return to the surface, resting in subterranean camps along the way.

world's **deepest cave**

VERONKINA

the deepest point on land
DENMAN GLACIER

The deepest point on land has been discovered under the Denman Glacier in East Antarctica. Deep below the Antarctic ice sheet, which is 1.3 miles thick on average, there is an ice-filled canyon whose floor is 11,500 feet below sea level. By comparison, the lowest clearly visible point on land is in the Jordan Rift Valley, on the shore of the Dead Sea, just 1,412 feet below sea level. It makes the Denman canyon the deepest canyon on land. Only trenches at the bottom of the ocean are deeper. The floor of the deepest —the Mariana Trench—is close to 7 miles below the sea's surface.

world's greatest number of geysers
YELLOWSTONE NATIONAL PARK

There are about 1,000 geysers that erupt worldwide, and 540 of them are in Yellowstone National Park, USA. That's the greatest concentration of geysers on Earth. The most famous is Old Faithful, which spews out a cloud of steam and hot water to a maximum height of 185 feet every 44 to 125 minutes. Yellowstone's spectacular water display is due to its closeness to molten rock from Earth's mantle that rises up to the surface. One day the park could face an eruption 1,000 times as powerful as that of Mt. St. Helens in 1980.

GEYSER FIELDS
Number of geysers

Yellowstone, Idaho/Montana/Wyoming, USA: 540

Valley of Geysers, Kamchatka, Russia: 139

El Tatio, Andes, Chile: 84

Orakei Korako, New Zealand: 33

Hveravellir, Iceland: 16

29,029 feet

Mount Everest's snowy peak is an unbelievable 5.5 miles above sea level. This mega mountain is located in the Himalayas, on the border between Tibet and Nepal. The mountain acquired its official name from surveyor Sir George Everest, but local people know it as Chomolungma (Tibet) or Sagarmatha (Nepal). In 1953, Sir Edmund Hillary and Tenzing Norgay were the first to reach its summit. Now more than 650 people per year manage to make the spectacular climb.

MOUNT EVEREST is earth's tallest mountain above sea level

WORLD'S TALLEST MOUNTAINS
Height above sea level in feet

Everest: 29,029

K2 (Qogir): 28,251

Kanchenjunga: 28,179

Lhotse: 27,940

Makalu: 27,838

world's longest
barrier
REEF

Australia's Great Barrier Reef is the only living thing that's clearly visible from space. It stretches along the Queensland coast for 1,400 miles, making it the largest coral reef system in the world. The reef is home to an astounding number of animals: over 600 species of corals alone, 133 species of sharks and rays, and 30 species of whales and dolphins. In recent years, climate change has posed a huge threat to the world's coral reefs, with rising sea temperatures causing areas to die off. The northern half of the Great Barrier Reef suffered particularly in 2016, and scientists fear that more damage is yet to come.

WORLD'S LONGEST BARRIER REEFS
Length in miles

Great Barrier Reef, Australia: 1,400

New Caledonia Barrier Reef, South Pacific: 930

Mesoamerican Barrier Reef, Caribbean: 620

Ningaloo Reef, Western Australia: 162

world's largest
hot desert
SAHARA DESERT

Sahara means simply "great desert," and great it is: It is the largest hot desert on the planet. It's almost the same size as the United States or China and dominates North Africa from the Atlantic Ocean in the west to the Red Sea in the east. It's extremely dry, with most of the Sahara receiving less than 0.1 inches of rain a year, and some places none at all for several years. It is stiflingly hot, up to 122°F, making it one of the hottest and driest regions in the world.

WORLD'S LARGEST HOT DESERTS
Size in square miles

Sahara Desert, North Africa: 3.63 million

Arabian Desert, Western Asia: 900,000

Great Victoria Desert, Australia: 250,000

Kalahari Desert, Africa: 220,000

Syrian Desert, Western Asia: 190,000

world's largest lake
CASPIAN SEA

Russia, Kazakhstan, Turkmenistan, Iran, and Azerbaijan border the vast Caspian Sea, the largest inland body of water on Earth. Once part of an ancient sea, the lake became landlocked between five and ten million years ago, with occasional fills of salt water as sea levels fluctuated over time. Now it has a surface area of about 149,200 square miles and is home to one of the world's most valuable fish: the beluga sturgeon, the source of beluga caviar, which costs up to $2,250 per pound.

WORLD'S LARGEST LAKES
Area in square miles

Caspian Sea, Europe/ Asia: 149,200

Lake Superior, North America: 31,700

Lake Victoria, Africa: 26,600

Lake Huron, North America: 23,000

Lake Michigan, North America: 22,300

NILE RIVER

world's longest river

People who study rivers cannot agree on the Nile's source—nobody knows where it actually starts. Some say the most likely source is the Kagera River in Burundi, which is the farthest headstream (a stream that is the source of a river) to flow into Lake Victoria. From the lake, the Nile proper heads north across eastern Africa for 4,132 miles to the Mediterranean. Its water is crucial to people living along its banks. They use it to irrigate precious crops, generate electricity, and, in the lower reaches, as a river highway.

WORLD'S LONGEST RIVERS
Length in miles

Yellow River, China: 3,395

Mississippi–Missouri river system, USA: 3,710

Yangtze River, China: 3,915

Amazon River, South America: 4,000

Nile River, Africa: 4,132

world's oldest
meteor crater

YARRABUBBA CRATER

The oldest known meteor crater on Earth has been identified in Western Australia. The Yarrabubba Crater is 2.229 billion years old. The impact might have altered the world's climate, bringing an end to an early global freeze known as "Snowball Earth." The strike gave rise to a crater about 40 miles across, which would have sent two hundred billion tons of vaporized ice into the atmosphere. Water vapor is a greenhouse gas, so the planet would have warmed quickly and considerably. However, nobody is really sure that Earth was covered in ice at that time. If not, the impact would have had the opposite effect: Dust sent up into the atmosphere would have cooled the planet.

weather
trending

AMAZON BURNING
STARS SPEAK OUT
Celebrities took to social media in 2019 to try to raise awareness about wildfires ravaging the Amazon rain forests. Much of this attention was aimed at Brazil, as environmental activists blamed its president, Jair Bolsonaro, for encouraging ranchers, loggers, and farmers to burn the Brazilian rain forest to clear land. Soccer star Cristiano Ronaldo and actor Leonardo DiCaprio were among the stars pressuring the Brazilian leader to take responsibility for the destruction.

#HURRICANEDORIAN
SOCIAL MEDIA SAVIORS

Hurricane Dorian hit the Bahamas in September 2019 as the worst natural disaster in the country's history. However, one positive aspect of the event is that it showed how social media can help people survive tough times. While the government scrambled to coordinate aid, Instagrammers shared stories of locals using boats to free trapped citizens, coordinated rescues, and posted information on where to go for real help. Social media also proved essential for people outside the Bahamas who requested information on the safety and whereabouts of their loved ones.

#SHOWYOURSTRIPES
CLIMATE DATA MADE EASY

Prof. Ed Hawkins at the National Centre for Atmospheric Science, University of Reading, designed a "warming stripes" graph in 2018 to show historic climate change in Wales. In 2019 he established a website where people can download a similar visualization for their own cities. The site had more than a million downloads in its first two months, with the design used everywhere from newspaper covers to weathermen's ties.

LIGHTNING KING
MOST STRIKING STATE

The state of Texas was named Lightning King of 2019 by Earth Networks Total Lightning Network (ENTLN), whose data showed it as the state with the highest level of lightning activity—an amazing 16,032,609 strikes, nearly double that of the next-highest state, Kansas, which had 8,200,321. Texas's high number stems in part from its massive size. The majority (83 percent) of the strikes recorded were in-cloud lightning rather than cloud-to-ground lightning.

ICE HOUSE
FAMILY HOME FROZEN

A beach house in Pulaski, New York, was encased in four feet of ice in 2019. A combination of high winds, sea spray, and freezing temperatures turned Maureen Morgan Whelan's summer home on the shores of Lake Ontario into an impenetrable ice fortress. Family members had to chip away bit by bit to avoid water damage to the house when the ice melted.

Antarctica's record high
SEYMOUR ISLAND

On February 9, 2020, the air temperature on Seymour Island, off the northernmost tip of the Antarctic Peninsula, was 69.35°F, the highest temperature ever recorded in Antarctica. Brazilian scientists witnessed the record-breaking summer temperature at their Marambio research station. The revelation followed three days after a record of 64.9°F was experienced at the research station at Esperanza. It follows the warmest January in Antarctica since records began. The peninsula is one of the fastest-warming regions on Earth, with the average air temperature having risen by 5.4°F during the past fifty years.

world's largest ice sculpture
ICE HOTEL

Want to sleep on a bed made of ice in subzero temperatures? That is the prospect for guests at the world's largest ice sculpture—the original Icehotel and art exhibition in Jukkasjärvi, 125 miles north of the Arctic Circle in Sweden. Here, the walls, floors, and ceilings of the sixty-five rooms are made of ice from the local Torne River and snow from the surrounding land. The beds, chairs, and tables—and even the bar and the drinks glasses standing on it—are made of ice. A neighboring ice church hosts one hundred weddings each winter. The hotel is open from December to April, after which it melts back into the wild.

OTHER ICE HOTELS
SnowCastle of Kemi, Finland
Hôtel de Glace, Quebec City, Canada
Bjorli Ice Lodge, Norway
Hotel of Ice at Bâlea Lac, Romania
Ice Village, Shimukappu, Japan

bushfire **most devastating** season
AUSTRALIA
2019–2020

Bushfires are an annual event in Australia, but 2019–2020 marked the country's most devastating season in half a century. By November 2019, blazes swept through the states of New South Wales, Victoria, Queensland, South Australia, Western Australia, and Tasmania. They were mostly brought under control in February 2020, when heavy rains helped firefighters to contain them. The fires laid waste to a staggering 46 million acres of bush, forest, and parks across the country. More than 3,000 properties burned to the ground, thirty-four people lost their lives, and an estimated one billion wild and domestic animals died as a result of the fires.

2019–2020 BUSHFIRE STATS

11 inches

Total spring rainfall across the whole country

107.4°F

Hottest day on record in Australia

14,500,000

Australians directly affected by the blaze

2.4 billion

Estimated cost in US dollars

KOALA CONCERN

The koala is the national symbol of Australia. Global awareness of the tragedy unfolding in Australia focused on the plight of these marsupials, an estimated 8,000 of which are believed to have perished in the fires. Koalas climb up to the crowns of trees to escape fire, but stood little chance of survival in blazes as fierce as these.

most intense
storm to hit land
HAIYAN

Typhoon Haiyan is one of the most powerful storms ever recorded and was the strongest-ever tropical storm to hit land. On November 8, 2013, it struck the Philippines, where it was known as Super Typhoon Yolanda.

Wind speeds reached 195 miles per hour, and vast areas of the islands were damaged or destroyed. Around eleven million people were affected: Many were made homeless, and at least 6,300 people were killed.

America's most
costly tornado
THE JOPLIN TORNADO

On May 22, 2011, a multiple-vortex tornado about one mile wide swept through Joplin, Missouri, killing 161 people and injuring more than one thousand others. It was the deadliest tornado in the United States since the 1947 Glazier-Higgins-Woodward tornadoes that swept across Texas, Kansas, and Oklahoma costing 181 people their lives. The Joplin tornado was by far the costliest tornado in U.S. history with $2.8 billion's worth of damage. It was registered as an EF5 category tornado—the most intense kind—with winds in excess of 200 miles per hour. It ripped houses off their foundations and lifted cars and trucks into the air.

highest tsunami in the United States LITUYA BAY

On July 9, 1958, a severe 7.8 magnitude earthquake triggered a huge rockslide into the narrow inlet of Lituya Bay, Alaska. The sudden displacement of water caused a mega tsunami, with a crest estimated to be 98 feet tall. The giant wave traveled across the bay and destroyed vegetation up to 1,722 feet above sea level. Five people died, and nearby settlements, docks, and boats were damaged. It was the highest tsunami to be recorded in the United States in modern times.

most destructive
storm surge in the United States

When Hurricane Katrina slammed into the Louisiana coast in 2005, a storm surge drove the sea almost 12.5 miles inland. New Orleans's hurricane surge protection was breached in fifty-three places, levees failed, boats and barges rammed buildings, and the city and countless neighboring communities were severely flooded. About 80 percent of New Orleans was underwater, close to 1,833 people lost their lives, and an area almost the size of the United Kingdom was devastated. The damage cost an estimated $108 billion. The U.S. Homeland Security secretary described the aftermath of the hurricane as "probably the worst catastrophe, or set of catastrophes" in the country's history.

HURRICANE KATRINA

MOST POWERFUL HURRICANES IN THE UNITED STATES
Wind speed in miles per hour

Labor Day Hurricane (1935): 185

Hurricane Andrew (1992): 177

Hurricane Katrina (2005): 175

Galveston Hurricane (1900): 145

hottest year on record 2016

Data gathered by NASA's Goddard Institute for Space Studies shows that 2016 was the warmest year since records began in 1880. Global average temperatures were 1.78°F warmer than they were in the mid-twentieth century, and it was the third year in a row that global temperature records were broken, continuing a long-term warming trend. Most scientists agree that this temperature increase is caused by a rise in the greenhouse gas carbon dioxide and other human-made emissions in the atmosphere.

most snowfall
in the United States

The greatest depth of snow on record in the United States occurred at Tamarack, near the Bear Valley ski resort in California, on March 11, 1911. The snow reached an incredible 37.8 feet deep. Tamarack also holds the record for the most snowfall in a single month, with 32.5 feet in January 1911. Mount Shasta, California, had the most snowfall in a single storm with 15.75 feet falling from February 13–19, 1959. The most snow in twenty-four hours was a snowfall of 6.3 feet at Silver Lake, Colorado, on April 14–15, 1921.

CALIFORNIA AND COLORADO

world's largest
hailstone,
VIVIAN,
South Dakota,

In August 2010, the town of Vivian, South Dakota, was bombarded by some of the biggest hailstones ever to have fallen out of the sky. They went straight through roofs of houses, smashed car windshields, and stripped vegetation. Among them was a world record breaker, a hailstone the size of a volleyball. It was 8 inches in diameter and weighed 2.2 pounds.

the world's
wettest place
MAWSYNRAM

Mawsynram is a cluster of villages in the Khasi Hills of India. The plateau on which they sit overlooks the vast flatlands of Bangladesh. With 467.4 inches of rain falling each year on average, Mawsynram is considered to be the wettest place on Earth. Life here is not without its problems.

Wooden bridges are washed away frequently, so locals build living bridges of knotted and interwoven roots of Indian rubber trees. People traditionally kept themselves dry with special umbrellas, called "knups." Woven from reeds, they kept the whole body dry.

DANCING CONGRESSWOMAN
AOC HAS MOVES!

Alexandria Ocasio-Cortez became the youngest woman ever elected to Congress in 2018. The day before she was sworn in, however, an old college video surfaced. Possibly released as a smear campaign, it featured Ocasio-Cortez and friends at Boston University eight years earlier re-creating iconic dances from popular 1980s films. Instead of embarrassing Ocasio-Cortez, the video made her more popular.

#STORMAREA51
AN UNLIKELY FACEBOOK EVENT

Area 51, a U.S. Air Force base and restricted military site in Nevada long rumored to contain classified information about alien activity, was in the news in 2019. More than two million people jokingly confirmed their attendance at a Facebook event named "Storm Area 51, They Can't Stop All of Us," with plans to break into the base. In fact some 6,000 people went to nearby Rachel, Nevada, for a festival called Alienstock.

ALOHA ISLANDS
THE HAPPIEST STATE
Hawai'i was rated America's happiest state in 2019 by WalletHub, whose study analyzed factors such as weather, working hours, job security, and depression rates. Hawai'i, known for its stunning scenery, came in first largely thanks to its no. 1 ranking for "Emotional & Physical Well-Being." The other states in the top five were Utah, Minnesota, California, and New Jersey.

WELCOME TO THE FUTURE
A NEWBORN FOR SAN DIEGO
The San Diego Zoo welcomed a new member of the family in 2019 with the birth of the zoo's 100th southern white rhinoceros. Shortly after the birth, San Diego announced the female calf's name: Future. The zoo hopes to use its southern white rhino genes to help bring back the northern white rhino from near extinction. Only two northerns remain in the wild and both are female.

LATER GATOR
UNEXPECTED VISITOR
Vacationers in Florida had the fright of their lives when they discovered a live alligator lounging on their alligator-shaped pool float outside their Miami Airbnb. They took a video of their unexpected visitor and shared it online. The alligator, which wasn't quite as big as his floating doppelgänger, soaked up the sun for a while before a wildlife manager took him away.

state with the oldest **Mardi Gras celebration**

ALABAMA

French settlers held the first American Mardi Gras in Mobile, Alabama, in 1703. Yearly celebrations continued until the Civil War and began again in 1866. Today 800,000 people gather in the city during the vibrant two-week festival. Dozens of parades with colorful floats and marching bands wind through the streets each day. Partygoers attend masked balls and other lively events sponsored by the city's social societies. On Mardi Gras, which means "Fat Tuesday" in French, six parades continue the party until the stroke of midnight, which marks the end of the year's festivities and the beginning of Lent.

state with the most
pilots per capita
ALASKA

Alaska is the only state in the United States in which more than 1 percent of citizens have a pilot's license—no surprise, considering Alaska has many islands and is the largest and most sparsely populated state. If you think this means the state has a surplus of skilled aviators, think again: Despite having six times the national average of pilots per capita, newspapers reported in 2016 that a pilot shortage in Alaska led the state to consider turning to drone technology. Many of its pilots and mechanics leave the state for high-flying careers in the lower forty-eight states.

MOST PILOTS PER CAPITA
Number of pilots per 100 people

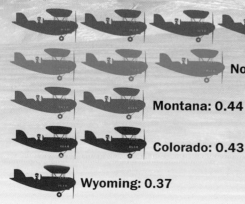

Alaska: 1.278

North Dakota: 0.476

Montana: 0.44

Colorado: 0.43

Wyoming: 0.37

state with the best-preserved
meteor crater
ARIZONA

Fifty thousand years ago, a meteor traveling at 26,000 miles per hour struck the earth near present-day Winslow, Arizona, to create a mile-wide, 550-foot-deep crater. Today, Meteor Crater is a popular tourist destination and is overseen by stewards who work to educate visitors about its formation. There is even an animated movie showing how it happened. The crater is sometimes known as the Barringer Crater, in recognition of mining engineer Daniel Moreau Barringer, who was the one to propose that it had been made by a meteorite. Previously, geologists had believed that the crater was a natural landform created over time.

only state where
diamonds are mined
ARKANSAS

Crater of Diamonds, near Murfreesboro, Arkansas, is the only active commercial diamond mine in the United States. Farmer and former owner John Wesley Huddleston first discovered diamonds there in August 1906, and a diamond rush overwhelmed the area after he sold the property to a mining company. For a time, there were two competing mines in this area, but in 1969, General Earth Minerals bought both mines to run them as private tourist attractions. Since 1972, the land has been owned by the state of Arkansas, which designated the area as Crater of Diamonds State Park. Visitors can pay a fee to search through plowed fields in the hope of discovering a gem for themselves.

most devoted
theme-park fan
CALIFORNIA

On June 22, 2017, forty-four-year-old Jeff Reitz completed two thousand consecutive daily visits to the Disneyland and California Adventure Park in Anaheim, California. After finding himself unemployed, the air force veteran bought an annual pass to the theme park in a bid to cheer himself up. That was on January 1, 2012, and Jeff continued to visit the park every single day thereafter. His favorite ride is the Matterhorn, a mountain-themed roller coaster on which passengers ride the rails in bobsleds. In March 2020, when the theme park faced temporary closure due to the Covid-19 pandemic, Reitz made his 2995th visit before drawing his mammoth visiting spree to an end.

state with the largest
elk population
COLORADO

Colorado is currently home to around 280,000 elk, making it the state with the largest elk population. Elk live on both public and private land across the state, from the mountainous regions to lower terrain. Popular targets for hunting, these creatures are regulated by both the Colorado Parks and Wildlife department and the National Park Service. Many elk live within the boundaries of Colorado's Rocky Mountain National Park. Elk are among the largest members of the deer family, and the males—called bulls—are distinguishable by their majestic antlers.

only state to manufacture
PEZ candy
CONNECTICUT

The PEZ factory in Orange, Connecticut, is the only place in the United States to make the world-famous candy. In 1927, an Austrian named Eduard Haas III invented PEZ as a breath mint. The letters come from the German word for peppermint, *Pfefferminz* (PfeffErminZ). The candy came to the United States in 1952, and the company opened its U.S. factory in 1975. Today, Americans consume an incredible three billion PEZ candies per year. The visitor center in Orange displays the largest collection of PEZ memorabilia on public display in the world, including the world's largest dispenser and a PEZ motorcycle.

horseshoe crabs
DELAWARE

Delaware Bay has the largest American horseshoe crab (*Limulus polyphemus*) population in the world. These creatures can be seen in large numbers on the bay's beaches in the spring. They appear during high tides on new and full moons, when they come onto land to spawn (deposit eggs). Horseshoe crabs have changed very little in the past 250 million years, and have therefore been called "living fossils." It is impossible to know the exact number of horseshoe crabs in the region, so every spring, volunteers at some of the state's beaches conduct counts to track spawning activity. In 2019, the Delaware Center for the Inland Bays estimated a record seasonal count of 2,105,447 horseshoe crabs on its beaches, peaking at 454,151 on May 20.

state with the most-visited amusement park
FLORIDA

Walt Disney World, in Lake Buena Vista, Florida, is home to several parks, including Magic Kingdom, the most-visited amusement park in the United States. Disney parks dominate the most-visited list, taking four of the top five spots. Magic Kingdom sees just over twenty million visitors from around the world who travel each year to ride the attractions, watch parades, and meet their favorite Disney characters. Divided into six themed areas, arguably the most iconic part of the park is Cinderella's Castle, which is illuminated each night by an impressive fireworks display and light-projection show.

MOST VISITED AMUSEMENT PARKS
Number of visitors per year in millions

Magic Kingdom, Walt Disney World, Florida: 20.9

Disneyland, California: 18.7

Tokyo Disneyland, Japan: 17.9

Tokyo DisneySea, Japan: 14.7

Universal Studios, Japan 14.3

state with the largest
Sports Hall of Fame
GEORGIA

At 43,000 square feet, Georgia's Sports Hall of Fame honors the state's greatest sports stars and coaches. The museum includes 14,000 square feet of exhibition space and a 205-seat theater. It owns more than 3,000 artifacts and memorabilia from Georgia's professional, college, and amateur athletes. At least 1,000 of these artifacts are on display at any time. The Hall of Fame corridor features over 300 inductees, such as golf legend Bobby Jones, baseball hero Jackie Robinson, and Olympic track medalist Wyomia Tyus.

only state with
a royal palace
HAWAII

Iolani Palace, in downtown Honolulu, is the only official royal residence in the United States. The palace was built from 1879–1882 by King Kalakaua, inspired by the styles of the grand castles of Europe. The monarchs did not live there for long, however: In 1893, the kingdom of Hawaii was overthrown by U.S. forces.

Kalakaua's sister, Queen Liliuokalani, was even held prisoner in the palace in 1895 following a plot to put her back on the throne. Iolani Palace was used as a government building until it became a National Historic Landmark in 1962. Restored to its nineteenth-century condition, it is now open to the public as a museum.

first state with a blue football field

Boise State's Albertsons Stadium, originally dubbed the "Smurf Turf" and now nicknamed "The Blue," was the first blue football field in the United States. In 1986, when the time came to upgrade the old turf, athletics director Gene Bleymaier realized that they would be spending a lot of money on the new field, yet most spectators wouldn't notice the difference. So, he asked AstroTurf to create the new field in the school's colors. Since the field's creation, students at the school have consistently voted for blue turf each time the field has been upgraded. Today, five more teams have opted for a colored playing field, including Eastern Washington, whose red field is dubbed "The Inferno," and Central Arkansas, where the teams play on purple and gray stripes.

IDAHO

state with the oldest
free public zoo
ILLINOIS

Lincoln Park Zoo, in Chicago, Illinois, remains the oldest free public zoo in the United States. Founded in 1868—nine years after the Philadelphia Zoo, the country's oldest zoo overall—Lincoln Park Zoo does not charge admission fees. More than two-thirds of the money for the zoo's operating budget comes from food, retail, parking, and fund-raising events. Nonetheless, the zoo continues to grow. In November 2016, it opened a new exhibit—the Walter Family Arctic Tundra—to house its newest addition: a seven-year-old male polar bear named Siku.

Kovler
LION HOUSE

the first
professional
baseball game

INDIANA

On May 4, 1871, the first National Association professional baseball game took place on Hamilton Field in Fort Wayne, Indiana. The home team, the Kekiongas, took on Forest City of Cleveland, beating them 2–0 against the odds. The Kekiongas were a little-known team at the time. In fact, this first game had been scheduled to take place between better-known Washington Olympic Club and the Cincinnati Red Stockings in Washington, D.C., on May 3. Heavy rain forced a cancellation, however, and so history was made at Fort Wayne the following day.

state with the shortest, steepest railroad
IOWA

At only 296 feet long, Fenelon Place Elevator in Dubuque, Iowa, is the shortest railroad in the United States, and its elevation of 189 feet also makes it the steepest. The original railway was built in 1882 by businessman and former mayor J. K. Graves, who lived at the top of the Mississippi River bluff and wanted a quicker commute down into the town below. Today's railway, modernized in 1977, is open to the public. It costs $1.50 for an adult one-way trip and consists of two quaint house-shaped cars traveling in opposite directions on parallel tracks.

state with the most rock concretions

KANSAS

Rock City, in Minneapolis, Kansas, boasts two hundred concretions of Dakota sandstone across a 5-acre park. They are the largest concretions in one place anywhere in the world. These concretions are huge spheres of rock, some of which measure up to 27 feet in diameter. They were created underground millions of years ago, when minerals deposited by water gradually formed hard, strong shells around small bits of matter in the sandstone. Over time, as the surrounding sandstone wore down, the concretions survived. Today, Rock City is a registered National Natural Landmark, and visitors can explore the park and climb the concretions for a $3.00 fee.

KENTUCKY

state with the biggest
fireworks display

The Kentucky Derby is the longest-running sporting event in the United States. It's also accompanied by the biggest fireworks display held annually in the United States—"Thunder Over Louisville"—which kicks off the racing festivities. Zambelli Fireworks, the display's creator, says that the show requires nearly 60 tons of fireworks shells and a massive 700 miles of wire cable to sync the fireworks to music. The theme for the 2019 firework display was "The Wonderful World of Thunder." In 2020, the fireworks show was canceled due to the Covid-19 pandemic; however, it is slated to resume in 2021.

state with the most crawfish
LOUISIANA

The majority of the crawfish consumed in the United States are caught in the state of Louisiana. While these critters may look like tiny lobsters, crawfish are actually freshwater shellfish and are abundant in the mud of the state's bayous—sometimes they are called "mudbugs." Before white settlers arrived in Louisiana, crawfish were a favorite food of the native tribes, who caught them using reeds baited with venison. Today, crawfish are both commercially farmed and caught in their natural habitat. The industry yields between 120 and 150 million pounds of crawfish a year, and the crustaceans are an integral part of the state's culture, with backyard crawfish boils remaining a popular local tradition.

state with the oldest state fair

MAINE

SKOWHEGAN STATE FAIR 1880

In January 1819, the Somerset Central Agricultural Society sponsored the first-ever Skowhegan State Fair. In the 1800s, state fairs were important places for farmers to gather and learn about new agricultural methods and equipment. After Maine became a state in 1820, the fair continued to grow in size and popularity, gaining its official name in 1842. Today, the Skowhegan State Fair welcomes more than 7,000 exhibitors and 100,000 visitors. Enthusiasts can watch events that include livestock competitions, tractor pulling, a demolition derby, and much more during the ten-day show.

state with the oldest
capitol building
MARYLAND

The Maryland State House in Annapolis is both the oldest capitol building in continuous legislative use and the only state house once to have been used as the national capitol. The Continental Congress met there from 1783–1784, and it was where George Washington formally resigned as commander in chief of the army following the American Revolution. The current building is the third to be erected on that site, and was actually incomplete when the Continental Congress met there in 1783, despite the cornerstone being laid in 1772. The interior of the building was finished in 1797, but not without tragedy—plasterer Thomas Dance fell to his death while working on the dome in 1793.

OLDEST CAPITOL BUILDINGS IN 2020
Age of building (year work was started)

Maryland: 248 years (1772)

Virginia: 235 years (1785)

New Jersey: 228 years (1792)

Massachusetts: 225 years (1795)

New Hampshire: 204 years (1816)

**state with
the oldest
Thanksgiving
celebration**

MASSACHUSETTS

The first Thanksgiving celebration took place in 1621, in Plymouth, Massachusetts, when the Pilgrims held a feast to celebrate the harvest. They shared their meal with the native Wampanoag people from a nearby village. While the celebration became widespread in the Northeast in the late seventeenth century,

Thanksgiving was not celebrated nationally until 1863, when magazine editor Sarah Josepha Hale's writings convinced President Abraham Lincoln to make it a national holiday. Today, Plymouth, Massachusetts, holds a weekend-long celebration honoring its history: the America's Hometown Thanksgiving Celebration.

most magical

state

MICHIGAN

Colon, Michigan, is known as the magic capital of the world. The small town is home to Abbott Magic Company—one of the biggest manufacturers of magic supplies in the United States—as well as an annual magic festival, magicians' walk of fame, and Colon Lakeside Cemetery, in which twenty-eight magicians are buried. The Abbott plant boasts 50,000 square feet dedicated to creating new tricks—from simple silk scarves to custom illusions. It is the only building in the world expressly built for the purpose of making magic.

state with
the largest

mall

MINNESOTA

The biggest shopping and entertainment center in the United States is the Mall of America in Bloomington, Minnesota. Spread over 5.4 million square feet with 12,000 parking spaces, it attracts forty million people a year. As well as the 500 retail units, the mall also contains the Nickelodeon Universe indoor amusement park and an aquarium. Minnesota is also considered the birthplace of the modern shopping mall as it is home to Southdale Center in Edina, one of the first malls, which opened in 1956.

MISSISSIPPI

only state to hold the International Ballet Competition

Every four years, Jackson, Mississippi, hosts the USA International Ballet Competition, a two-week Olympic-style event that awards gold, silver, and bronze medals. The competition began in 1964 in Varna, Bulgaria, and rotated among the cities of Varna; Moscow, Russia; and Tokyo, Japan. In June 1979, the competition came to the United States for the first time, and, in 1982, Congress passed a Joint Resolution designating Jackson as the official home of the competition. In addition to medals, dancers vie for cash prizes and the chance to join established ballet companies.

America's first ice-cream cone

MISSOURI

It is said that America's first ice-cream cone was introduced through chance inspiration at the St. Louis World's Fair in 1904. According to the most popular story, a Syrian salesman named Ernest Hamwi saw that an ice-cream vendor had plenty of ice cream but not enough cups and spoons to serve it. Seeing that a neighboring vendor was selling waffle cookies, Hamwi took a cookie and rolled it into a cone for holding ice cream. An immediate success, Hamwi's invention was hailed by vendors as a "cornucopia"—an exotic word for a "cone."

state with the most
T. rex specimens

The first *Tyrannosaurus rex* fossil ever found was discovered in Montana—paleontologist Barnum Brown excavated it in the Hell Creek Formation in 1902. Since then, many major T. rex finds have been in Montana—from the "Wankel Rex," discovered in 1988, to "Trix," discovered in 2013.

Another T. rex fossil was uncovered in Montana in 2016: "Tufts-Love Rex," named for paleontologists Jason Love and Luke Tufts, was found about 20 percent intact at the site in Hell Creek. Today, the Museum of the Rockies in Bozeman, Montana, houses thirteen T. rex specimens—more than anywhere else in the world.

MONTANA

state with the largest indoor rain forest

NEBRASKA

The Lied Jungle at Henry Doorly Zoo in Omaha, Nebraska, features three rain forest habitats: one each from South America, Africa, and Asia. At 123,000 square feet, this indoor rain forest is larger than two football fields. It measures 80 feet tall, making it as tall as an eight-story building. The Lied Jungle opened in 1992 and cost $15 million to create.

Seven waterfalls rank among its spectacular features. Ninety different animal species live here, including saki monkeys, pygmy hippos, and many reptiles and birds. Exotic plant life includes the African sausage tree, the chocolate tree, and rare orchids. The zoo's other major exhibit—the Desert Dome—is the world's largest indoor desert.

state that produces
the most gold
NEVADA

Although it has been called the "Silver State" for its silver production, Nevada is also the state that produces the most gold. According to the Nevada Mining Association, Nevada produces more than three-quarters of America's gold and accounts for 5.4 percent of world gold production. Gold can be found in every county of Nevada, although it is not always accessible to casual prospectors. Nevada's Carlin Trend is rich in gold deposits—and is, in fact, the world's second-largest gold resource—but the deposits are so finely spread that they require an expensive process to extract the precious mineral.

state with the oldest skiing club NEW HAMPSHIRE

Nansen Ski Club, in Milan, New Hampshire, was founded by Norwegian immigrants in 1872, making it the oldest continuously operating skiing club in the United States. When it first opened, the venue only accepted other Scandinavians living in the area but was then made available to everyone as more skiing enthusiasts began to move into New Hampshire from Quebec, to work in the mills there. For fifty years, the club was home to the largest ski jump east of the Mississippi, and was used for Olympic tryouts.

state with the most
diners
NEW JERSEY

The state of New Jersey has more than six hundred diners, earning it the title of "Diner Capital of the World." The state has a higher concentration of diners than anywhere else in the United States. They are such an iconic part of the state's identity that, in 2016, a New Jersey diners exhibit opened at Middlesex County Museum, showcasing the history of the diner from early twentieth-century lunch cars to modern roadside spots. The state has many different types of diners, including famous restaurant-style eateries like Tops in East Newark, as well as retro hole-in-the-wall diners with jukeboxes and faded booths.

state that made the world's largest
flat enchilada
NEW MEXICO

New Mexico was home to the world's largest flat enchilada in October 2014, during the Whole Enchilada Fiesta in Las Cruces. The record-breaking enchilada measured 10.5 feet in diameter and required 250 pounds of masa dough, 175 pounds of cheese, 75 gallons of red chili sauce, 50 pounds of onions, and 175 gallons of oil. Led by Roberto's Mexican Restaurant, the making—and eating—of the giant enchilada was a tradition at the festival for thirty-four years before enchilada master Roberto Estrada hung up his apron in 2015.

America's smallest church

NEW YORK

The smallest church in America, Oneida's Cross Island Chapel, measures 81 by 51 inches and has just enough room for the minister and two churchgoers. Built in 1989, the church is in an odd location, in the middle of a pond. The simple, whitewashed clapboard chapel stands on a little jetty that has moorings for a boat or two. The island that the chapel is named for barely breaks the surface of the water nearby and is simply a craggy pile of rock bearing a cross.

state with the largest
private house
NORTH CAROLINA

The Biltmore Estate, in the mountains of Asheville, North Carolina, is home to Biltmore House, the largest privately owned house in the United States. George Vanderbilt commissioned the 250-room French Renaissance–style chateau in 1889, and opened it to his friends and family as a country retreat in 1895. Designed by architect Richard Morris Hunt, Biltmore House has an impressive thirty-five bedrooms and forty-three bathrooms, and boasts a floor space of over four acres. In 1930, the Vanderbilt family opened Biltmore House to the public.

LARGEST PRIVATE HOUSES IN THE U.S.
Area in square feet

Biltmore House, Asheville, NC: 175,000

Oheka Castle, Huntington, NY: 109,000

Sydell Miller Mansion, Palm Beach, FL: 84,626

Pensmore, Highlandville, MO: 72,215

Rennert Mansion, Sagaponack, NY: 66,400

biggest honey producer
NORTH DAKOTA

For the last fourteen years, North Dakota has outstripped all other U.S. states in the production of honey. Currently, there are 485,000 honey-producing colonies in North Dakota, and in 2018, they produced more than 38.2 million pounds of the sweet stuff. It seems the North Dakota climate is just right for honeybees and—more important—for the flowers from which they collect their nectar. Typical summer weather features warm days but cool nights.

first laws protecting working women
OHIO

In the 1800s, working conditions in U.S. factories were grueling and pay was very low. Most of the workers were women, and it was not uncommon for them to work for twelve to fourteen hours a day, six days a week. The factories were not heated or air-conditioned and there was no compensation for being sick.

By the 1850s, several organizations had formed to improve the working conditions for women and to shorten their workday. In 1852, Ohio passed a law limiting the working day to ten hours for women under the age of eighteen. It was a small step, but it was also the first act of legislation of its kind in the United States.

state with the largest
multiple-arch dam
OKLAHOMA

Completed in 1940, the Pensacola Dam in Oklahoma is 6,565 feet long, making it the longest multiple-arch dam in the world. The dam stretches across the Grand River and controls the 43,500 acres of water that form the Grand Lake o' the Cherokees.

The massive structure is a towering 145 feet tall and consists of no fewer than 535,000 cubic yards of concrete, about 655,000 barrels of cement, 75,000 pounds of copper, and a weighty 10 million pounds of structural steel.

world's largest
cinnamon roll
OREGON

Wolferman's Gourmet Baked Goods holds the record for the largest cinnamon roll ever made. The spiced confection measured 9 feet long and was topped with 147 pounds of cream cheese frosting. It was made to celebrate the launch of the bakery's new 5-pound cinnamon roll. Using its popular recipe, Wolferman's needed 20 pounds of eggs, 350 pounds of flour, 378 pounds of cinnamon-sugar filling, and no fewer than 220 cinnamon sticks in their scaled-up version. The 1,150-pound cinnamon roll was transported to Medford's Annual Pear Blossom Festival in south Oregon, where visitors snapped it up for $2 a slice.

the most crayons
PENNSYLVANIA

Easton, Pennsylvania, is home to the Crayola crayon factory and has been the company's headquarters since 1976. The factory produces an amazing twelve million crayons every single day, made from uncolored paraffin and pigment powder.

In 1996, the company opened the Crayola Experience in downtown Easton. The Experience includes a live interactive show in which guests can watch a "crayonologist" make crayons, just as they are made at the factory nearby.

state with the oldest
Fourth of July celebration

RHODE ISLAND

Bristol, Rhode Island, holds America's longest continuously running Fourth of July celebration. The idea for the celebration came from Revolutionary War veteran Rev. Henry Wight, of Bristol's First Congregational Church, who organized "Patriotic Exercises" to honor the nation's founders and those who fought to establish the United States. Today, Bristol begins celebrating the holiday on June 14, and puts on a wide array of events leading up to the Fourth itself—including free concerts, a baseball game, a Fourth of July Ball, and a half marathon.

state with
the hottest
pepper
SOUTH CAROLINA

Pepper X, created by Smokin' Ed Currie of Rock Hill, South Carolina, is the hottest pepper in the world, measuring an average of 3.18 million Scoville heat units (SHU). To get a feel for how hot that is, just know that a regular jalapeño clocks in at 10,000 to 20,000 SHU. Currie also created the world's third-hottest chili, the Carolina Reaper. The Reaper held the record from 2013 to 2017, before being beaten by the 2.4 million SHU Dragon's Breath pepper in May. Just four months after that, Currie's Pepper X took the chili pepper world by storm.

WORLD'S HOTTEST PEPPERS
By peak heat in millions of SHU

Pepper X: 3.18

Dragon's Breath: 2.4

Carolina Reaper: 2.2

Trinidad Moruga Scorpion: 2

Brain Strain: 1.9

state with the largest
sculpture
SOUTH DAKOTA

While South Dakota is famous as the home of Mount Rushmore, it is also the location of another giant mountain carving: the Crazy Horse Memorial. The mountain carving, which is still in progress, will be the largest sculpture in the world when it is completed, at 563 feet tall and 641 feet long. Korczak Ziolkowski, who worked on Mount Rushmore, began the carving in 1948 to pay tribute to Crazy Horse—the Lakota Sioux leader who defeated General Custer at the Battle of the Little Bighorn. Nearly seventy years later, Ziolkowski's family continues his work, relying completely on funding from visitors and donors.

state that makes all the
MoonPies
TENNESSEE

Tennessee is the home of the MoonPie, which was conceived there in 1917 by bakery salesman Earl Mitchell Sr. after a group of local miners asked for a filling treat "as big as the moon." Made from marshmallow, graham crackers, and chocolate, the sandwich cookies were soon being mass-produced at Tennessee's Chattanooga Bakery, and MoonPie was registered as a trademark by the bakery in 1919. MoonPies first sold at just five cents each and quickly became popular— even being named the official snack of NASCAR in the late 1990s. Today, Chattanooga Bakery makes nearly a million MoonPies every day.

TEXAS

largest urban bat colony

If you want to see a sky filled with hundreds of thousands of bats, head to Austin, Texas, any time from mid-March to November. The city's Ann W. Richards Congress Avenue Bridge is home to the world's largest urban bat colony—roughly 1.5 million bats in all. The Mexican free-tailed bats first settled here in the 1980s, and numbers have grown steadily since. They currently produce around 750,000 pups per year. These days the bats are a tourist attraction that draws about 140,000 visitors to the city, many of them hoping to catch the moment at dusk when large numbers of bats fly out from under the bridge to look for food.

HYATT

state with the largest
saltwater lake
UTAH

The Great Salt Lake, which inspired the name of Utah's largest city, is the largest saltwater lake in the United States, at around 75 miles long and 35 miles wide. Sometimes called "America's Dead Sea," it is typically larger than each of the states of Delaware and Rhode Island. Its size, however, fluctuates as water levels rise and fall: Since 1849, the water level has varied by as much as 20 feet, which can shift the shoreline by up to 15 miles. Great Salt Lake is too salty to support most aquatic life but is home to several kinds of algae as well as the brine shrimp that feed on them.

state that produces the most
maple syrup
VERMONT

The state of Vermont produced a total of 2.07 million gallons of maple syrup in 2019, an increase of 7 percent on the previous year. Vermont's more than 1,500 maple syrup producers take sap from six million tree taps. They have to collect 40 gallons of maple sap in order to produce just 1 gallon of syrup. Producers also use maple sap for making other treats, such as maple butter, sugar, and candies.

state with the largest
office building
VIRGINIA

The Pentagon—the headquarters of the United States Department of Defense—is America's largest office building. The five-sided structure, which was completed in 1943 after just sixteen months of work, cost $83 million to build. It contains 3.7 million square feet of office space—triple the amount of floor space in the Empire State Building—as well as a large central courtyard. Despite containing 17.5 miles of corridors, the building's design means that a person can walk from any point to another in about 7 minutes. There are currently 24,000 employees, both military and civilian, working in the building.

The Teapot Dome Service Station in Zillah, Washington, was once the oldest working gas station in the United States, and is still the only one built to commemorate a political scandal. Now preserved as a museum, the gas station was built in 1922 as a monument to the Teapot Dome Scandal, in which Albert Fall, President Warren G. Harding's secretary of the interior, took bribes to lease government oil reserves to private companies. The gas station, located on Washington's Old Highway 12, was moved in 1978 to make way for Interstate 82, then again in 2007 when it was purchased by the City of Zillah as a historic landmark.

state with the oldest
gas station
WASHINGTON

state with the longest
steel arch bridge
WEST VIRGINIA

The New River Gorge Bridge in Fayetteville spans 3,030 feet and is 876 feet above the New River. It is both the longest and largest steel arch bridge in the United States. Builders used 88 million pounds of steel and concrete to construct it. The $37 million structure took three years to complete and opened on October 22, 1977. Bridge Day, held every October since 1980, is a BASE-jumping event at the New River Gorge Bridge. Hundreds of BASE jumpers and about 80,000 spectators gather for the one-day festival. Among the most popular events is the Big Way, in which large groups of people jump off the bridge together. During Bridge Day 2013, Donald Cripps became one of the world's oldest BASE jumpers, at eighty-four years old.

largest
cross-country
ski race
WISCONSIN

Each year in February, Wisconsin hosts America's largest cross-country ski race. The race attracts over 10,000 skiers, all attempting to complete the 55-kilometer (34-mile) course from Cable to Hayward. Milestones along the way include Boedecker Hill, Mosquito Brook, and Hatchery Park.

The event is part of the Worldloppet circuit of twenty ski marathons across the globe. The winner of the 2018 race, Benjamin Saxton from Lakeville, Minnesota, completed the course in two hours, forty-seven minutes, and thirty-five seconds to claim the $7,500 prize money.

Grand Prismatic Spring, in Yellowstone National Park in Wyoming, is the largest hot spring in the United States. The spring measures 370 feet in diameter and is more than 121 feet deep; Yellowstone National Park says that the spring is bigger than a football field and deeper than a ten-story building. Grand Prismatic is not just the largest spring but also the most photographed thermal feature in Yellowstone due to its bright colors. The colors come from different kinds of bacteria, living in each part of the spring, that thrive at various temperatures. As water comes up from the middle of the spring, it is too hot to support most bacterial life, but as the water spreads out to the edges of the spring, it cools in concentric circles.

sports
STARS

sports stars
trending

RUNNING MOM
WINNINGEST WORLD CHAMP
In September 2019, American sprinter Allyson Felix broke Jamaican legend Usain Bolt's record for most IAAF World Championship medals after winning gold in the mixed-gender 4x400-meter relay. She achieved this stunning feat only ten months after the difficult birth of her first child, coming back from her break to a season in which she was named to the U.S. Olympic team for the fifth time.

#WETHENORTH
RAPTORS WIN BIG
The Toronto Raptors beat the Golden State Warriors in the 2018–19 NBA finals, bringing the Larry O'Brien Trophy to Canada for the first time. They beat the two-time returning champions by 114–110 in game six of the NBA finals. Canadian rapper Drake, who is a Raptors global ambassador and superfan, released two singles to celebrate: "Omertà" and "Money In The Grave."

EMBARRASSING DADS
LAYING DOWN THE RULES

Fifteen-year-old U.S. tennis star Coco Gauff made headlines in 2019 for jokingly scolding her dad during a break between sets at the Auckland Open. Her father Corey Gauff, also her coach, used a mild cuss word that was caught by his mic and broadcast on live television. The video of his daughter telling him to apologize went viral, prompting viewers to comment on the coach becoming the coached.

NEYMAR
MOST TWEETED-ABOUT ATHLETE

According to ESPN, Brazilian footballer Neymar was the most-discussed athlete on Twitter in 2019. The traffic was probably a result of the close eye football fans kept on Neymar's hotly anticipated trade from Paris Saint-Germain (PSG) back to his former club Barcelona, which ultimately fell through. One of the most sought-after footballers in the world, Neymar received a €36.8 million (U.S.$41m) contract when he moved to PSG in 2017.

MR. AVOCADO
F1 FAN SLIP GOES VIRAL

Australian Formula 1 driver Daniel Ricciardo became the subject of a viral meme during the 2019 Australian Grand Prix after a young fan got the racer's name wrong during an interview with a local news channel. The fan, five-year-old Louis Pope, called the driver "Danny Avocado," leading fans to photoshop Ricciardo as the green fruit. Pope and Ricciardo later met for an interview, with the young fan clutching an avocado.

world's highest
BASE jump
from a
building

FRED FUGEN AND VINCE REFFET

BASE jumping is just about the world's most terrifying sport to watch. BASE stands for the types of places a person may jump from: Buildings, Antennae, Spans (usually bridges), and Earth (usually cliffs). In April 2014, French daredevils Fred Fugen and Vince Reffet set a new record by jumping from a specially built platform at the top of the world's tallest building, the Burj Khalifa in Dubai. They jumped from a height of 2,716 feet, 6 inches. The highest ever BASE jump was performed by Russian Valery Rozov from 23,690 feet high on the north side of Mount Everest. He landed safely on the Rongbuk Glacier at an altitude of 19,520 feet, some 4,100 feet below.

world's highest
tightrope walk

Tightrope walking looks hard enough a few feet above the ground, but Swiss stuntman Freddy Nock took it to the next level when he walked between two mountains in the Swiss Alps in March 2015. On a rope set 11,590 feet above sea level, Freddy took about thirty-nine minutes to walk the 1,140 feet across to the neighboring peak. The previous record had held since 1974, when Frenchman Philippe Petit walked between the Twin Towers of New York's former World Trade Center.

FREDDY NOCK

world's longest
skateboard
ramp jump
DANNY
WAY

Many extreme sports activities are showcased at the annual X Games and Winter X Games. At the 2004 X Games, held in Los Angeles, skateboarder Danny Way set an amazing record that remains unbeaten. On June 19, Way made a long-distance jump of 79 feet, beating his own 2003 world record (75 feet). In 2005, he jumped over the Great Wall of China. He made the jump despite having torn ligaments in his ankle during a practice jump on the previous day.

jockey with the most
Triple Crown wins

EDDIE ARCARO

Many horse-racing experts think that Eddie Arcaro was the best-ever American jockey. Arcaro rode his first winner in 1932, and by the time of his retirement thirty years later, he had won the Triple Crown twice, in 1941 and 1948. He also won more Triple Crown races than any other jockey, although Bill Hartack has equaled Arcaro's total of five successes in the Kentucky Derby. Arcaro won 4,779 races overall in his career.

JOCKEYS WITH MULTIPLE WINS IN TRIPLE CROWN RACES
Number of wins (years active)

Jockey	Number of wins	Years active
Eddie Arcaro	17	1932–1957
Bill Shoemaker	11	1955–1986
Earl Sande	9	1921–1930
Bill Hartack	9	1956–1969
Pat Day	9	1985–2000
Gary Stevens	9	1988–2013

world's highest basketball shot

HOW RIDICULOUS

Australian trick-shot group How Ridiculous continues to break its own record. In 2015, one member made a basket from an amazing 415 feet, but the group has since improved that distance several times. In January 2018, How Ridiculous achieved its most astonishing feat yet: a basket from 660 feet, 10 inches. The group made the record shot at Maletsunyane Falls, Lesotho, in southern Africa, after five days of setup work and practice. How Ridiculous is a group of three friends who started trying trick shots for fun in their backyards in 2009. They now have a successful YouTube channel and business and are also involved in Christian charitable work.

NBA team

with the most championship titles

BOSTON CELTICS

The Boston Celtics top the NBA winners' list with seventeen championship titles out of twenty-one appearances in the finals, just one title more than the Los Angeles Lakers. The two teams have met twelve times in the finals, resulting in nine wins for the Celtics. The best years for the Boston Celtics were the 1960s, with 1967 being the only year in the decade that they did not bring the championship home.

NBA CHAMPIONSHIP WINS		
Boston Celtics	17	1957–2008
LA Lakers	16	1949–2010
Golden State Warriors	6	1947–2018
Chicago Bulls	6	1991–1998
San Antonio Spurs	5	1999–2014

most career points
in the NBA

KAREEM
ABDUL-JABBAR

Many fans regard Kareem Abdul-Jabbar as the greatest-ever basketball player. He was known by his birth name, Lew Alcindor, until 1971, when he changed his name after converting to Islam. That same year he led the Milwaukee Bucks to the team's first NBA championship title. As well as being the all-time highest scorer of points during his professional career with a total of 38,387, Abdul-Jabbar also won the NBA Most Valuable Player (MVP) award a record six times.

NBA MOST CAREER POINTS LEADERS
Number of points

Kareem Abdul-Jabbar	38,387
Karl Malone	36,928
LeBron James	34,087
Kobe Bryant	33,643
Michael Jordan	32,292

youngest NBA player to reach 30,000 career points

LEBRON JAMES

On Tuesday, January 23, 2018, aged thirty-three years and twenty-four days, LeBron James became the youngest player in NBA history to reach 30,000 points, smashing Kobe Bryant's previous record. A year later, in February 2019, James reached 32,000 points. He overtook Bryant in the career scoring list in early 2020, just one day before Bryant died in an aircraft accident. The two had become friends in recent months and James, having spoken to Bryant the night before, was devastated by the news.

DIANA TAURASI

WNBA player with the most career points

MOST CAREER POINTS IN THE WNBA
Number of points

Diana Taurasi	8,575
Tina Thompson	7,488
Tamika Catchings	7,380
Cappie Pondexter	6,811
Katie Smith	6,452
Candice Dupree	6,452

After a standout college career and three NCAA championships with the University of Connecticut Huskies, Diana Taurasi joined the Phoenix Mercury in the WNBA in 2004. Her prolific scoring helped the Mercury to their first WNBA title in 2007 (and two more since then), and her international career includes four consecutive Team USA Olympic golds, 2004–16. Playing mainly as guard, Taurasi became the all-time leading WNBA scorer in 2017.

most valuable
football team
DALLAS COWBOYS

It has been more than twenty years since the Dallas Cowboys won the Super Bowl, yet the team has been the most valuable in the NFL for thirteen straight seasons up to 2019. The team was most recently valued at $5 billion. Cowboys' owner Jerry Jones paid what now seems a bargain $150 million for the franchise in 1989. In recent years, broadcast and stadium revenues in the NFL have soared.

NFL TEAM VALUATIONS
Revenue in billions of U.S. dollars
(as of September 2019)

Dallas Cowboys	5.0
New England Patriots	3.8
New York Giants	3.3
Los Angeles Rams	3.2
Washington	3.1

NFL player with the most
career touchdowns
JERRY RICE

Jerry Rice is generally regarded as the greatest wide receiver in NFL history. He played in the NFL for twenty seasons—fifteen of them with the San Francisco 49ers—and won three Super Bowl rings. As well as leading the career touchdowns list with 208, Rice also holds the "most yards gained" mark with 23,546 yards. Most of his touchdowns were from pass receptions (197), often working with the great 49ers quarterback Joe Montana.

NFL PLAYERS WITH THE MOST CAREER TOUCHDOWNS
Number of touchdowns (career years)

Jerry Rice	208	1985–2004
Emmitt Smith	175	1990–2004
LaDainian Tomlinson	162	2001–2011
Terrell Owens	156	1996–2010
Randy Moss	156	1998–2012

DREW BREES

Drew Brees is one of the greatest quarterbacks of all time. After a stellar college career at Purdue, he spent five seasons with the San Diego Chargers before joining the New Orleans Saints in 2006. He was still starring with the Saints in 2018, setting a new season's record for pass completion percentage, which he then nearly beat in 2019. He has now recorded six of the best eight pass completion seasons in NFL history. As well as total pass completions and completion percentage, Brees holds NFL records for career passing yards and career touchdown passes.

NFL PLAYERS WITH THE MOST CAREER TOUCHDOWNS
Number of touchdowns (career years)

Drew Brees	6,867	2001–2019
Tom Brady	6,377	2000–2019
Brett Favre	6,300	1991–2010
Peyton Manning	6,125	1998–2015
Dan Marino	4,967	1983–1999

NFL team with the most Super Bowl appearances

Founded in 1959 as one of the members of the new American Football League, the then-Boston Patriots struggled for many years. They only made their first Super Bowl appearance in 1985, when they lost to the Bears, but in recent years they have been the NFL's dominant force. Led by veteran quarterback Tom Brady and coach Bill Belichick, they played in four out of five Super Bowls, 2014–18, and won three of them. They are now tied with the Steelers for most Super Bowl successes but well ahead of all the others with eleven appearances in total.

NEW ENGLAND PATRIOTS

NFL TEAMS WITH THE MOST SUPER BOWL WINS
Number of wins

Team	Number of wins	Super Bowls
New England Patriots	6	Super Bowls XXXVI, XXXVIII, XXXIX, XLIX, LI, LIII
Pittsburgh Steelers	6	Super Bowls IX, X, XIII, XIV, XL, XLIII
San Francisco 49ers	5	Super Bowls XVI, XIX, XXIII, XXIV, XXIX
Dallas Cowboys	5	Super Bowls VI, XII, XXVII, XXVIII, XXX
Green Bay Packers	4	Super Bowls I, II, XXXI, XLV
New York Giants	4	Super Bowls XXI, XXV, XLII, XLVI

school with most
Rose Bowl wins

The Rose Bowl is college football's oldest postseason event, first played in 1902. Taking place near January 1 of each year, the game is normally played between the Pac-12 Conference champion and the Big Ten Conference champion, but one year in three it is part of college football's playoffs. The University of Southern California has easily the best record in the Rose Bowl, with twenty-five wins from thirty-four appearances, followed by the Michigan Wolverines (eight wins from twenty). The Oregon Ducks defeated the Wisconsin Badgers 28–27 in the 2020 game. This was the Oregon Ducks' fourth Rose Bowl success.

USC TROJANS

MLB team with the most World Series wins

NEW YORK YANKEES

WORLD SERIES WINS
Number of wins

New York Yankees	27	1923–2009
St. Louis Cardinals	11	1926–2011
Oakland Athletics*	9	1910–1989
Boston Red Sox**	9	1903–2018
San Francisco Giants***	8	1905–2014

* Previously played in Kansas City and Philadelphia

** Originally Boston Americans

*** Previously played in New York

The New York Yankees are far and away the most successful team in World Series history. Since baseball's championship was first contested in 1903, the Yankees have appeared forty times and won on twenty-seven occasions. The Yankees' greatest years were from the 1930s through the 1950s, when the team was led by legends like Babe Ruth and Joe DiMaggio. Nearest challengers are the St. Louis Cardinals from the National League with eleven wins from nineteen appearances.

longest

World Series championship drought

The 2016 World Series saw a dramatic showdown between the two Major League Baseball clubs with the longest World Series droughts: the Chicago Cubs and the Cleveland Indians. The Cubs had been one of baseball's most successful teams in the early years of the World Series at the start of the twentieth century, but between 1908 and 1945, they lost the World Series seven times. Following that string of World Series losses, the team scarcely won even a divisional title until 2016—the year the drought finally ended. The Cubs clinched the World Series title in the tenth inning in the deciding seventh game.

CHICAGO CUBS, broken 2016

WORLD SERIES DROUGHTS

Team	Last World Series win	Last appearance in World Series
Cleveland Indians	1948	2016
Texas Rangers	Never (since 1961*)	2011
Milwaukee Brewers	Never (since 1969*)	1982
San Diego Padres	Never (since 1969*)	1998

MLB player with the highest
batting average

HIGHEST CAREER BATTING AVERAGES
Batting average (career years)

Ty Cobb	.366	1905–1928
Rogers Hornsby	.359	1915–1937
Shoeless Joe Jackson	.356	1908–1920
Lefty O'Doul	.349	1919–1934
Ed Delahanty	.346	1888–1903

TY COBB

Ty Cobb's batting average of .366 is one of the longest-lasting records in Major League Baseball. In reaching that mark, Cobb, known to fans as "The Georgia Peach," astonishingly batted .300 or better in twenty-three consecutive seasons, mainly with the Detroit Tigers. Cobb's status in the game was made clear when he easily topped the selection poll for the first set of inductees into the Baseball Hall of Fame.

CAREER HOME RUNS
Number of home runs (career years)

Barry Bonds	762	1986–2007
Hank Aaron	755	1954–1976
Babe Ruth	714	1914–1935
Alex Rodriguez	696	1994–2016
Willie Mays	660	1951–1973

Barry Bonds's power hitting and skill in the outfield rank him as a five-tool player—someone with good speed and baserunning skills, who is also good at hitting the ball, fielding, and throwing. He played his first **seven** seasons with the Pittsburgh Pirates before moving to the San Francisco Giants for the next twelve seasons. He not only holds the record for most career home runs, but also for the single-season record of seventy-three home runs, which was set in 2001. Barry's godfather is Willie Mays, the first player ever to hit 300 career home runs and steal 300 bases.

BARRY
BONDS

BECK
47

CHRIS WONDOLOWSKI

MLS player with the most regular-season goals

Californian Chris Wondolowski took a while to get his professional soccer career going. He was drafted by the San Francisco Earthquakes in a late round in 2005 but didn't earn a regular starting spot with the Quakes until 2010. Since then, however, he has scored more than ten goals for San Francisco every season up to 2019. His total stood at 159 going into the 2020 season, which he says will be his last. He has also earned thirty-five appearances for the U.S. Men's National Team, including two at the 2014 World Cup in Brazil.

MLS REGULAR-SEASON TOP SCORERS
Number of goals (career years)

Chris Wondolowski	159	(2005–)
Landon Donovan	145	(2001–2016)
Jeff Cunningham	134	(1998–2011)
Jaime Moreno	133	(1996–2010)
Kei Kamara	127	(2006–)

country with the most
FIFA World Cup wins
BRAZIL

Brazil, host of the 2014 FIFA World Cup, has lifted the trophy the most times in the tournament's history. Second on the list, Germany, has more runners-up and semifinal appearances and hence, arguably, a stronger record overall. However, many would say that Brazil's 1970 lineup, led by the incomparable Pelé, ranks as the finest team ever. The host team has won five of the twenty tournaments that have been completed to date.

FIFA WORLD CUP WINNERS
Number of wins

Brazil	5	1958, 1962, 1970, 1994, 2002
Germany*	4	1954, 1974, 1990, 2014
Italy	4	1934, 1938, 1982, 2006
Uruguay	2	1930, 1950
Argentina	2	1978, 1986
France	2	1998, 2018

* As West Germany
1954, 1974

sports stars

country with the most

FIFA Women's World Cup wins

UNITED STATES

In 1991, the first Women's World Cup was held, in which the USA beat Norway 2–1 in the final. Since then, the United States has won the tournament three times more. Megan Rapinoe was named the best player of the tournament following the USA's 2019 triumph. She scored the team's second goal in the 2–0 victory over the Netherlands in the final.

FIFA WOMEN'S WORLD CUP WINNERS
Number of wins

United States	4	1991, 1999, 2015, 2019
Germany	2	2003, 2007
Norway	1	1995
Japan	1	2011

KRISTINE LILLY

woman with the most international soccer caps

In her long and successful career, Kristine Lilly played club soccer principally with the Boston Breakers. When she made her debut on the U.S. national team in 1987, however, she was still in high school. Her total of 354 international caps is the world's highest for a man or woman and her trophy haul includes two World Cup winner's medals and two Olympic golds.

WOMEN WITH THE MOST INTERNATIONAL SOCCER CAPS
Number of caps (career years)

Kristine Lilly, USA	354	1987–2010
Christie Pearce, USA	311	1997–2015
Christine Sinclair, Canada	296	2000–
Mia Hamm, USA	276	1987–2004
Julie Foudy, USA	272	1988–2004

lowest-winning score
in a major golf tournament

In Gee Chun of South Korea is still in the early stages of her professional career but has already achieved two wins in the five annual women's golf "majors." Most remarkable of all was her achievement at the 2016 Evian Championship: the lowest score in a major championship by any player, male or female, at twenty-one under par. The previous women's record was nineteen under par, shared by five players, while two players share the men's record of twenty under par.

IN GEE CHUN

PGA golfer with lowest
season average
2019 RORY McILROY

Northern Ireland's Rory McIlroy recorded his first professional tournament win as a nineteen-year-old in 2009, and only had to wait until 2011 for his first major title, the U.S. Open. Since then, he has won three more majors and enjoyed extensive spells at the top of the world rankings. The 2019 season, though without a win in one of the majors, was one of his best. McIlroy took the Vardon Trophy and the Byron Nelson Award for the lowest-scoring player in PGA golf, repeating his successes of 2012 and 2014.

woman with the most
Grand Slam titles
MARGARET COURT

The Grand Slam tournaments are the four most important tennis events of the year: the Australian Open, the French Open, Wimbledon, and the U.S. Open. The dominant force in women's tennis throughout the 1960s and into the 1970s, Australia's Margaret Court heads the all-time singles list with twenty-four, although Serena Williams may beat this. Court won an amazing sixty-four Grand Slam titles in singles, women's doubles, and mixed doubles, a total that seems unlikely to be beaten.

TOTAL GRAND SLAM TITLES
Number of titles (singles) (years active)

Name	Titles	Years active
Margaret Court, Australia	64 (24)	1960–1975
Martina Navratilova, Czech/USA	59 (18)	1974–2006
Serena Williams, USA	39 (23)	1998–
Billie Jean King, USA	39 (12)	1961–1980
Margaret Osborne duPont, USA	37 (6)	1941–1962

man with the most
Grand Slam singles titles

With twenty wins, Swiss tennis star Roger Federer stands at the top of the all-time rankings in Grand Slam tennis singles tournaments. His best tournament has been Wimbledon, which he has won eight times. Federer did not win a Grand Slam between 2012 and 2017, partly due to injury troubles. In 2017, however, after a break for knee surgery, he was back and as good as ever, with wins in Australia (repeated in 2018) and at Wimbledon.

ROGER FEDERER

GRAND SLAM SINGLES WINS
Number of wins (years active)

Player	Number of wins	Years active
Roger Federer, Switzerland	20	1998–
Rafael Nadal, Spain	19	2001–
Novak Djokovic, Serbia	17	2003–
Pete Sampras, USA	14	1988–2002
Roy Emerson, Australia	12	1961–1973

most consecutive NASCAR championship wins

JIMMIE JOHNSON

The NASCAR drivers' championship has been contested since 1949. California native Jimmie Johnson is tied at the top of the all-time wins list with seven, but his five-season streak, 2006–10, is easily the best in the sport's history. Johnson's racing career began on 50cc motorcycles when he was just five years old. All of Johnson's NASCAR championship wins have been achieved driving Chevrolets; his current car is a Camaro ZL1. He has won eighty-three NASCAR races so far in his career but surely has more to come.

NASCAR CHAMPIONSHIP WINS
Number of wins (years in which the title was won)

Driver	Wins	Years
Jimmie Johnson	7	(2006, 2007, 2008, 2009, 2010, 2013, 2016)
Dale Earnhardt Sr.	7	(1980, 1986, 1987, 1990, 1991, 1993, 1994)
Richard Petty	7	(1964, 1967, 1971, 1972, 1974, 1975, 1979)
Jeff Gordon	4	(1995, 1997, 1998, 2001)

GRITTY

What's seven feet tall, bright orange, and has big eyes? It sounds like the start of a joke, but since his first appearance in September 2018 Gritty, the Philadelphia Flyers' mascot, has racked up hundreds of thousands of Twitter followers. Unusual among pro sports teams, the Flyers have only had a mascot for one season before, way back in the 1970s, but in his short life, Gritty has made up for this, showing up on TV talk shows and trending online. He was voted the number one mascot in the league by the NHL Players' Association in 2019.

NHL team with the most

Stanley Cup wins

MONTREAL CANADIENS

The Montreal Canadiens are the oldest and, by far, the most successful National Hockey League team. In its earliest years, the Stanley Cup had various formats, but since 1927, it has been awarded exclusively to the champion NHL team—and the Canadiens have won it roughly one year in every four. Their most successful years were the 1940s through the 1970s, when the team was inspired by all-time greats like Maurice Richard and Guy Lafleur.

STANLEY CUP WINNERS (SINCE 1915)
Number of wins (time span)

Montreal Canadiens	24	1916–1993
Toronto Maple Leafs	11	1918–1967
Detroit Red Wings	11	1936–2008
Boston Bruins	6	1929–2011
Chicago Blackhawks	6	1934–2015

NHL player with the most **career points**

WAYNE GRETZKY

Often called "The Great One," Wayne Gretzky is regarded as the most successful hockey player. As well as scoring more goals and assists than any other NHL player—both in regular-season and in postseason games—Gretzky held over sixty NHL records in all by the time of his retirement in 1999. The majority of these records still stand. Although he was unusually small for an NHL player, Gretzky had great skills and an uncanny ability to be in the right place at the right time.

NHL ALL-TIME HIGHEST REGULAR-SEASON SCORERS
Number of points (goals) (career years)

Wayne Gretzky	2,857 (894)	1978–1999
Jaromír Jágr	1,921 (766)	1990–2018
Mark Messier	1,887 (694)	1979–2004
Gordie Howe	1,850 (801)	1946–1979
Ron Francis	1,798 (549)	1981–2004

youngest-ever
NHL
captain

CONNOR
MCDAVID

At nineteen years old, center Connor McDavid was named team captain of the Edmonton Oilers at the beginning of the 2016–17 season. Remarkably, the season before that was his first in the NHL. McDavid has been hailed as the "Next One" (hockey's next household name). His value to the Oilers was made plain in 2017 when he signed a record $100 million, eight-year contract, to begin in 2018–19.

first
woman
to play
in an
NHL game
MANON
RHÉAUME

Manon Rhéaume had a fine career as a goaltender in women's ice hockey, earning World Championship gold medals with the Canadian National Women's Team. She is also the first—and only—woman to play for an NHL club. On September 23, 1992, she played one period for the Tampa Bay Lightning in an exhibition game against the St. Louis Blues, during which she saved seven of nine shots. She later played twenty-four games for various men's teams in the professional International Hockey League.

world's largest
cheerleading cheer
HANGZHOU
China

Cheerleading has a huge following around the world and is at the early stages of consideration as a possible Olympic sport. The city of Hangzhou in China staged the largest-ever cheerleading cheer in December 2018 with an astonishing 2,102 participants aged from five years old to sixty-eight. Hangzhou will be hosting the 2022 Asian Games and the event was part of the advance publicity for that championship.

most combined-event
gold medals in the Climbing World Championship

SEAN MCCOLL

Competition climbing will appear as an Olympic sport for the first time in 2021. Climbers compete on indoor climbing walls in three disciplines—lead, speed, and bouldering—to arrive at a combined score for a medal. Canada's Sean McColl has achieved three golds in the combined event (2012, 2014, 2016) at the World Championship, more than any other competitor to date. Austria's Jakob Schubert gained the 2018 title, however, and has since topped the world rankings. Slovenia's Janja Garnbret was the 2018 women's winner and is also world number one. But who will take the first-ever Olympic gold medals?

world's fastest
spin
on ice
skates
OLIVIA
RYBICKA-
OLIVER

Although only eleven years old at the time of her record-breaking performance, Olivia Rybicka-Oliver from Nova Scotia, Canada, achieved an astonishing spin rate of 342 revolutions per minute—over five per second. This smashed the previous record of 308 revolutions per minute. Olivia, who is Polish by birth, set her record in Warsaw on January 19, 2015. Her performance was part of a fund-raising event held by Poland's Fundacja Dziecięca Fantazja (Children's Fantasy Foundation) for terminally ill children.

first-ever skater
to land six quadruple jumps
NATHAN CHEN

Nathan Chen made skating history at the 2018 Winter Olympics by being the first-ever skater to attempt and land six quadruple jumps during one performance. Quad jumps—in which the skater spins around four times while in the air—are among the hardest moves in skating, and grouping several of them in one program makes them more difficult still. Chen's record-breaking Olympic performance did not earn him a medal because he had skated poorly earlier in the competition, but a few weeks later, he won the World Championship after landing his six quads once again.

most Winter Olympics
snowboarding gold medals
SHAUN WHITE

A professional skateboarder, successful musician, and Olympic and X Games star, Shaun White has an astonishing range of talents. He has won more X Games gold medals than anyone else, but his three Olympic golds, in the halfpipe competitions in 2006, 2010, and 2018, the most ever by a snowboarder, are perhaps his biggest achievement. The best of all was in 2018 when he landed two super-difficult back-to-back tricks in the final round to jump into first place. White's medal happened to be the USA's 100th at the Winter Olympics; that total now stands at 105, but Norway leads in that category with 132 to date.

most medals won by a nation in one Summer Olympics

USA

The record medal count of 239 (including 78 golds) has been held by the United States since the 1904 Games in St. Louis, Missouri. In those days, international travel was much more difficult than it is now—as a result, it's estimated that about 90 percent of the competitors were Americans! Just twelve countries competed and only ten countries won any medals. By comparison, 206 countries competed at Rio 2016.

won by an
most medals
individual

MICHAEL PHELPS

Michael Phelps may be the greatest competitive swimmer ever. He did not win any medals at his first Olympics in 2000, but at each of the Summer Games from 2004 through 2016, he was the most successful individual athlete of any nation. When he announced his retirement after London 2012, he was already the most decorated Olympic athlete ever—but he didn't stay retired for long. At Rio 2016, he won five more golds and a silver, taking his medal total to twenty-eight—twenty-three of them gold.

MOST SUCCESSFUL OLYMPIANS
Number of medals won (gold)

Michael Phelps	USA	Swimming	2004–16	28 (23)
Larisa Latynina	USSR	Gymnastics	1956–64	18 (9)
Nikolai Andrianov	USSR	Gymnastics	1972–80	15 (7)

Four athletes, Ole Einar Bjørndalen of Norway, Boris Shakhlin of the Soviet Union, Edoardo Mangiarotti of Italy, and Takashi Ono of Japan, have each won thirteen medals.

American gymnast ever

Simone Biles won her first two world championship titles in 2013 at the age of sixteen and has added to her total every season since then, apart from during a career break in 2017. Biles is only four foot eight, but her tiny frame is full of power and grace, displayed most memorably in her favorite floor exercise discipline. She is so good that several special moves are named after her—and they are so difficult that she is the only competitor so far to perform these in championships.
To date, she has won four Olympic and nineteen World Championship gold medals.

SIMONE BILES

fastest
man in the world
USAIN BOLT

Jamaica's top athlete Usain Bolt is the greatest track sprinter who has ever lived. Other brilliant Olympic finalists have described how all they can do is watch as Bolt almost disappears into the distance. Usain's greatest victories have been his triple Olympic gold medals at London 2012 and Rio 2016, plus two gold medals from Beijing 2008. Usain also holds the 100-meter world record (9.58s) and the 200-meter record (19.19s), both from the 2009 World Championships.

FASTEST 100-METER SPRINTS OF ALL TIME
Time in seconds

Usain Bolt (Jamaica)	9.58 Berlin 2009
Usain Bolt (Jamaica)	9.63 London 2012
Usain Bolt (Jamaica)	9.69 Beijing 2008
Tyson Gay (USA)	9.69 Shanghai 2009
Yohan Blake (Jamaica)	9.69 Lausanne 2012

most decorated
Paralympian ever
TRISCHA ZORN

Trischa Zorn is the most successful Paralympian of all time, having won an astonishing fifty-five medals, forty-one of them gold, at the Paralympic Games from 1980 to 2000. She won every Paralympic event she entered from 1980 to 1988. Zorn is blind and helps military veterans with disabilities enter the world of parasport. Zorn was inducted into the Paralympic Hall of Fame in 2012.

LEADING FEMALE PARALYMPIC MEDALISTS
Number of medals won

Trischa Zorn, USA	55
Béatrice Hess, France	25
Sarah Storey, Great Britain	25
Chantal Petitclerc, Canada	21
Mayumi Narita, Japan	20

country with the most
all-time Paralympic medals
USA

Although China topped the Paralympic medal table at the 2016 Summer Games in Rio (239 medals), with the United States coming in fourth (115 medals), the United States comfortably leads the all-time medal count in the Paralympic Summer Games. Norway heads the standings in the Winter Games, with the United States in second, giving the United States an overall medal total that will be unbeatable for many years to come.

COUNTRY WITH THE MOST PARALYMPIC MEDALS
Total number of medals won

United States	2,494
Germany*	1,871
Great Britain	1,824
Canada	1,220
France	1,209

* includes totals of former East and West Germany

first
Paralympic
triathlon

RIO 2016

Most people would find a 750-meter swim, followed by a 20-kilometer bike ride, then a 5-kilometer run quite challenging—but then try all that with a physical or visual impairment, too. That's how it is for paratriathletes. Sixty Paralympians qualified for the first-ever Olympic paratriathlon at Rio in 2016. Only six of the possible ten events (men and women) were contested in Rio, with the United States' two golds, one silver, and one bronze being the best national result.

index

Photo credits

David Forman/Media Bakery; 192 top: Agencia Estado/AP images; 192 bottom: Ramon Espinosa/AP images; 193 top: Ed Hawkings (University of Reading); 193 center: Mike Hardiman/iStock/Getty Images; 193 bottom: Natalie Kucko; 194: DEA/ DANI-JESKE/age fotostock; 195: Daniel Kreher/ imageBROKER/age fotostock; 196-197: Brett Hemmings/Getty Images; 197 icon: Kozyrevaelena/ Dreamstime; 198: Tigeryan/Getty Images; 199: eyecrave/Getty Images; 200: Michele Cornelius/ Dreamstime; 201: Everett Collection/age fotostock; 202: Imaginechina/Newscom; 203: CampPhoto/ Getty Images; 204: Nadine Spires/Dreamstime; 206-207: Mario Tama/Getty Images; 208 top: Susan Walsh/AP images; 208 bottom: Mario Tama/Getty Images; 209 top: Bill Bachmann/Pacific Stock/Media Bakery; 209 center: San Diego Zoo/MEGA/ Newscom; 209 bottom background: Minesh Shah/ Dreamstime; 210: Dan Anderson via ZUMA Wire/ Newscom; 211: Alaska Stock/age fotostock; 212: Russ Kinne/age fotostock; 214: Sam Gangwer/The Orange County Register/ZUMAPRESS.com/ Newscom; 215: aznature/Getty Images; 216: Randy Duchaine/Alamy Stock Photo; 217: Newman Mark/ age fotostock; 218: Dan Anderson/Getty Images; 220: Lucy Pemoni/AP images; 221: Steve Conner/ Icon SMI/Corbis/Getty Images; 223: Buyenlarge/ Getty Images; 224: Don Smetzer/Alamy Stock Photo; 225: Keith Kapple/Superstock, Inc.; 226: Stephen J. Cohen/Getty Images; 227: John Cancalosi/Pantheon/ Superstock, Inc.; 228: johnwoodcock/Getty Images; 233: Richard Finkelstein for the USA IBC; 234: Historic Collection/Alamy Stock Photo; 235: Edgloris E. Marys/age fotostock; 236: Robert_Ford/Getty Images; 237: Bob Thomason/The Image Bank/Getty Images; 238: Nansen Ski Club; 239: Loop Images/ UIG/Getty Images; 240: Visit Las Cruces; 241: Tina Pomposelli; 242: Alan Marler/AP images; 244: Library of Congress; 245: John Elk III/Lonely Planet Images/Getty Images; 246: Courtesy of Wolferman's Bakery™; 247: Matt Rourke/AP images; 248: Jerry Coli/Dreamstime; 249: Ed Currie/PuckerButt Pepper Company; 250: Sergio Pitamitz/age fotostock; 252: Fritz Poelking/age fotostock; 253: Johnny Adolphson/Dreamstime; 254: Tara Golden/Dreamstime; 256: Kevin Schafer/Photolibrary/Getty Images; 258: Tom Lynn/Sports Illustrated/Getty Images; 259: Richard Maschmeyer/age fotostock; 260-261: Chris Brown/Cal Sport Media/ZUMA Wire/AP images; 262 top: Patrick Smith/Getty Images; 262 bottom: Tom Szczerbowski/Getty Images; 263 top: Dave Rowland/Getty Images; 263 bottom left: Inna Kyselova/Dreamstime; 264: ZJAN/Supplied by WENN.com/Newscom; 266: Streeter Lecka/Getty Images; 267: AP images; 268: How Ridiculous; 269: Chris Sweda/Chicago Tribune/TNS/Getty Images; 270: Focus on Sport/Getty Images; 271: Mark J. Terrill/AP images; 272: Barry Gossage/NBAE/Getty Images; 273: Tom Szczerbowski/Getty Images; 274: Greg Trott/AP images; 277: Kevork Djansezian/Getty Images; 278: Jed Jacobsohn/Getty Images; 279: Jamie Squire/Getty Images; 280: Mark Rucker/ Transcendental Graphics/Getty Images; 281: Denis Poroy/AP images; 282: Scott Winters/Icon Sportswire/AP images; 283: AP images; 284: David Vincent/AP images; 285: Guang Niu/Getty Images; 286: Chatchai Somwat/Dreamstime; 288: Daily Express/Hulton Archive/Getty Images; 290: Jared C. Tilton/Getty Images; 291: Bruce Bennett/Getty Images; 292: The Canadian Press, Ryan Remiorz/AP images; 293: Rocky Widner/Getty Images; 294: Minas Panagiotakis/Getty Images; 295: Al Messerschmidt/AP images; 296: mhodges/Getty Images; 297: MIGUEL MEDINA/AFP/Getty Images; 298: David Madison/Photodisc/Getty Images; 299: MARCO BERTORELLO/AFP/Getty Images; 300: The Yomiuri Shimbun/AP images; 301: Popperfoto/Getty Images; 302: Mitchell Gunn/Dreamstime; 303: Zhukovsky/Dreamstime; 304: Stuart Robinson/ Express Newspapers/AP images; 305: ARIS MESSINIS/AFP/Getty Images; 306: Raphael Dias/ Getty Images; 307: Buda Mendes/Getty Images. All other photos © Shutterstock.com.

SCHOLASTIC SUMMER

READ-A-PALOOZA

⅀ READ · CELEBRATE · GIVE ⅀

Scholastic Summer Read-a-Palooza is a free program that unites communities in a nationwide campaign to celebrate reading for fun while improving access to books during the summer.

In 2020, the program offered a reimagined kids experience in Scholastic *Home Base*, a safe and free digital community for readers.

While in Scholastic *Home Base*, kids could visit the new Summer Read-a-Palooza Zone to read select e-books, meet their favorite authors, make new friends, keep Reading Streaks™ to unlock book donations, join dance parties and more!

By reading throughout the summer months and tracking their Reading Streaks™ in *Home Base*, kids helped donate 100,000 new print books from Scholastic!

Through a collaboration with United Way Worldwide, the donated titles were distributed across the country to locations where access to books was needed most.

Congratulations to all our participants on another amazing summer! Here are some impressive summer reading stats from the 2020 Scholastic Summer Read-a-Palooza:

64,000 THE NUMBER OF READING STREAKS™ CREATED BY KIDS TO HELP UNLOCK THE 100,000 DONATED PRINT BOOKS!

58,000 THE NUMBER OF TIMES KIDS VISITED THE SCHOLASTIC SUMMER READ-A-PALOOZA ZONE IN HOME BASE!

38 THE NUMBER OF UNITED WAY COMMUNITIES THAT RECEIVED AND DISTRIBUTED DONATED BOOKS!

From free e-books to author events, kids enjoyed the new Scholastic Summer Read-a-Palooza Zone in Home Base!

Congratulations to all the readers who kept their Reading Streaks™ this summer to help unlock the 100,000 print books!

SCHOLASTIC